Laug of the Damned

Mike Corbett

Centrifugal Publishing

Requests for permission to make copies of any part of this work should be mailed to Permissions Department, Centrifugal Publishing, PO Box 11874, Fort Lauderdale, FL 33339

ISBN: 978-0-9830679-0-0 PB
         978-0-9830679-1-7 eBook

Printed in the United States of America

Library of Congress Control Number: 2010939714

For Danielle.

TABLE OF CONTENTS

INTRODUCTION

Have you watched world news day after day and noted the persistent phenomena of helpless people quietly starving while an incompetent corporate pirate sits atop a golden toilet half a world away? Without a heaven and a hell to complete the job, the quality of justice merely inconveniences perpetrators while permitting victims to languish. This book is a consequence of the idea that most of us would like to see people get what they deserve.

Why would anyone be curious enough about my opinions to want such a book? That's the first of many relevant questions I had to ignore in order to achieve my goal of writing anything at all. Hah! Who was I trying to fool? Within hours, I began compromising my artistic isolation by worrying about rubbing people the wrong way.

Since it was my hope not to give offense, particularly regarding religious beliefs, this once mediocre idea had to be forced through a filter that reduced it to thin broth. To this exciting distillate I have introduced an abundance of meandering commentary and humor you can see coming a mile away.

Regarding the speculations about heaven and hell, if you were a teacher in a parochial school and wanted to maintain order and command attention, the threat of eternal pain in hell offers greater leverage against nonconformity than the promise of everlasting happiness. Kids take that for granted anyway. A good priest can give children nightmares worrying about abstractions that may or may not constitute sin. Moreover, the fear of burning in a fire produces disproportionately more vivid images than a vague concept like bliss, even if you're not nine years old. Misery is simply more eloquent.

Consider the various artistic representations of the two destinations. In the case of heaven, the Renaissance masters focused on the beauty and serenity of the main characters. There isn't much of a clue as to the cause of their satisfaction, but it may be obvious to the properly faithful. Hell, on the other hand, is graphically portrayed in art from all periods, so anyone can see what's making those unlucky residents uncomfortable. Even a few artists who didn't believe in God enjoyed taking a shot at eternal suffering.

I was surprised by the diversity of opinions that people shared with me regarding what, if anything, happens after death. I expected some differentiation based on faith, age, or nationality, but after hours of interviews, unexpectedly, it seemed that nearly everyone's concept of an afterlife was unique. To this challenging issue, I applied my modest ability to interpret and relate. I fortified the haphazard structure of largely unrelated essays by including the wisdom of many of history's great and not so great thinkers. They may directly or merely vaguely apply, but they would make interesting reading without my contribution.

To the interviews, I added a few biographies, and a hodgepodge of personal observations, with the intention of amusing the reader five minutes at a time. Oh yes, and I threw in an eight-act play to lend emphasis to the leitmotif.

If at some point you get the feeling that I am demonstrating a bias toward some particular belief or ideological preference, I urge you to suspend it. If I have, in the process, lost my objectivity, I have also sacrificed my right to hold any notion, no matter how seemingly preposterous, up to ridicule. I also admit to an infatuation with the English language that may have produced descriptive excesses and obscure references. Like Polonius, I may have been better served by more matter with less art.

Murray, who appears on the back cover as well as within some of the essays, is a good friend and source of ideas and inspiration. If he did not actually exist, he would have to be invented as a repository for the distribution of negative feedback. My latent cowardice requires the company of a kindred spirit.

If I may level a final criticism upon myself, it is that there are far too many related issues that have been unintentionally omitted. If you read this book and find it wanting, a thousand pages on the same subject by the same author will be unlikely to satisfy you, so don't be too concerned about a sequel.

Sale of film rights and an invitation to appear on Oprah or The Colbert Report seem remote, but my friends will all be expected to buy several copies. If I sold a hundred books, could I call myself an author? That's how I want to respond when someone asks what I do for a living. I haven't had a good answer to that question for decades.

BABYLON

Those who seek public office must be prepared to endure temptations most of us cannot possibly grasp. Satan works harder in Moscow, Buenos Aires, and Washington D.C. thanks to a confluence of vulnerabilities such as greed and incompetence. Virtually no one but His Demonic Highness can function effectively within the compromised decadence of power. This is according to plan.

When you, the newly elected, with your high moral standing and dreams of a better world arrive at the seat of government, you quickly learn how little can be accomplished without abandoning whatever quanta of morality* you claim to possess.

Everybody knows how the system works. You, as a state representative, for example, are seeking wetlands protection. In exchange for the realization of this admirable goal, you must agree to vote to extend relief from pollution enforcement. The industry that will benefit from this legislation produces employment and pays taxes that build highways and keep schools open. So far, so good. Your constituency wasn't expecting a Hyperion; they're just relieved you haven't been caught by the paparazzi with an under-

---

*Shedding your principles does not mean abandoning your ludicrous façade of integrity or religious beliefs. They are crucial to your advancement.

1

aged prostitute yet. The temptations are everywhere. When you start shaping and coloring your hair in the bizarre style that politicians must conform to, it is not simple vanity. It is the remarkable expectation that the freshman class of rosy-cheeked pages will think you look 25 years younger!

Since no office exists in perpetuity, your survival may depend on your adaptability. Your obligations to those who elected you will have to be shuffled in with your debts to your peers in office, and inconsequentially, with your sense of ethical purpose.

Having pandered your way through a multi-term career in politics, you are now sufficiently experienced to demonstrate your moral versatility by becoming a lobbyist. You don't get all the compensation lobbyists earn by embracing any standards but those of your corporate sponsor, so prepare yourself for some rhetorical gymnastics. A company that calls itself *Clear Skies* may derive the whole of its income from the production of a substance whose only effect is to kill rare birds (thus clearing the skies). Your job as spokesman for the bird-killing industry is to convince morally ambiguous legislators that the extinction of these avian pests will liberate their former habitat for profitable strip mining, and spare us the expense of endangered species protection. The savings can be redirected to urban centers where it can be used to bribe aldermen, inspectors and other minor functionaries.

Your previous identity as a human will of course dissolve, but your preposterous income will permit you to flee to the south of France and become a dark farceur or an Existentialist. Satan's ability as a choreographer is unchallenged in the halls of power, but I cannot fathom why he has allowed so many buildings in our Capital to be painted white. Maybe black or red (like High Plains Drifter*) would better suit his infernal taste.

> *"I had been told I was on the road to hell, but I had no idea it was just a mile down the road with a dome on it."*
>
> Abraham Lincoln

---

*In this Eastwood western gothic film, a mining town is painted red to signify its similarity to hell.

NINE BALL, CORNER POCKET

Fate is seldom thwarted by design, and intent transforms only the most superficial elements of our existence. We are rarely treated to an event that satisfies our appetite for universal justice and balance, and when it actually occurs, it is frequently disguised as irony. If it were possible to contrive a perfect transition for a politician to glide from public life, the following instance might represent it accurately.

Alben Barkley enjoyed a successful career as a United States Senator (Kentucky) and then vice president (under Truman). After a brief lunge at the presidency, he returned to the Senate where by all accounts, he served admirably. He was making a speech at Washington & Lee University where he was responding to a frequently asked question about his feelings regarding his apparent demotion to the back row of the Senate with the other junior Senators. He had, after all, enjoyed seniority previously, but had to be re-elected to the seat.

By good fortune, his reflections on this matter were captured on an audio recording and the listener can perceive his eloquence and sincerity. He had the enthusiasm and inflection of a southern preacher with long vowels and longer pauses for effect. At the conclusion of his oratory, he uttered these words: "And I am willing to be a junior. I'm glad to sit in the back row for I would rather be a servant in the house of the Lord than sit in the seats of the mighty." On the recording, you can then clearly hear a clatter of furniture and many concerned voices, since as everyone soon became aware, the honorable Mr. Barkley had just expired.

Remember, he was 78 years old, so his death could have been no great surprise, but the timing couldn't have been choreographed to create a soft landing strip for his soul with any more skill. You may not think politicians are always honest, but lying requires the sort of effort that elderly people are just too experienced to waste on it. In my family for example, the grandfolks, with trivial exceptions, have become tactlessly honest*.

Absent total candor, if he could be slick enough to fool heaven, I will allow myself to be persuaded. His passing permits us, if even momentarily, to cherish the belief that prayers can be answered in a timely fashion.

"To be in hell is to drift; to be in heaven is to steer."
George Bernard Shaw

---

*My implication that mendacity declines with age is based upon consultation with a number of geriatric professionals. The consensus is that aging is accompanied by increased frankness when the incentives of romantic, financial, or career enhancement are removed. Additionally, reduced memory function makes effective lying more difficult. Opportunistic or spontaneous lies are not likely to totally vanish with age, but we may hope for Mr. Barkley's sake that sincerity accompanied him to his ultimate destination.

WHAT ABOUT ANGELS?

Since hard evidence of their existence is scant, we must rely on religious literature, fortified by anecdotal evidence and faith, to infer their natures. The traditional image of a winged androgynous being with little or no body hair, and the genital configuration of a Ken doll may be fanciful. The utility of wings in heaven must be questioned, unless the atmosphere there is similar to that of our little blue planet. (If they have wings, they should have beaks and talons). There are many appendages that are appropriate to an earth-like environment that may be either exclusively decorative or absent in the upper climes. Teeth, feet, nipples, and courting tackle would be superfluous on an angel, so perhaps the traditionally beautiful representations should give way to a variety of possibilities. Some angels could be spectral or wraith-like, as a mist across the moor. Others could be as gargoyles, visually compelling but benign.

Others could be simpler yet; maybe a perfect sphere would inspire awe, or even a trapezoid. (God forbid!)

Since we aspirants are likely to be at the base of the pecking order, we should be prepared to greet angels and saints with appropriate humility. I can't fathom salaaming to a trapezoid, so I hope there's at least a tiara atop whatever it is to ennoble her, him, or it. (Pronouns may be a real dilemma up there.)

In the great battle between good and evil that preceded awareness, a few of God's perfect creations were cast into hell. Apparently, they backed the wrong side. Here, for the anatomically curious, one may find some of the unwanted scraps from heaven's denizens. Not only wings, but long noses, pointy ears, beards and other anthropomorphic remnants will be theatrically advantageous in hell. The addition of horns, hooves, and tails as essential parts of the devilish form suggests a fire sale at a sausage factory, but the dramatis personae need to accessorize.

> *I dreamed death came the other night*
> *And Heaven's gate swung wide.*
> *A glorious angel soon appeared*
> *And ushered me inside.*
> *And there to my astonishment*
> *Were folks I'd known on earth.*
> *Some I'd judged and found unfit*
> *And some of little worth.*
> *Indignant words rose to my lips*
> *But were never set free,*
> *For every face showed stunned surprise*
> *Not one expected me.*
>
> *Unknown*

SATAN'S OFFICE

ACT I

Satan:

Something's different around here. I don't hear sounds of wailing anymore.

Demon:

That's true, chief. Its slowly being replaced by grumbling and kvetching.

Satan:

Kvetching! This isn't a deli, it's eternal damnation!

Demon:

Apparently earth has become so miserable that hell's torments don't compare very favorably anymore. They still scream, but now its for hot towels.

Satan:

Tell 'em if they stop their infernal complaining, they can

have sexual intercourse once a
week.

Demon: Ever since that big nightclub
fire, they've been doing that
anyway. It seems the novelty of
sex in hell is like a kind of
"Mile High Club", and we can't
keep them off of one another.

Satan: Have you tried pouring molten
lava on them?

Demon: Naturally chief, but everything
we've tried so far has been in-
corporated into their ghastly
coupling rituals. The Marquis
de Sade is even hosting mix-
ers.

Satan: Maybe our design is becoming
obsolete. See what it would
cost to level the whole place
and start again.

Demon: I'm on it chief.

A MARRIED WOMAN

"'Til death do us part" is a limitation that a sizable number of respondents hope to exceed. A great relationship may be characterized by the term "soul mates", which carries the implication of an infinite union. Sounds pretty good, but I persuaded a female acquaintance to supplement my traditional male viewpoint with her insights on heaven, and I became aware of a few inconsistencies. I am tempted to the sin of envy as I listen to a woman describe a paradise with relatives everywhere, (especially mom & pop) assembled on a healthy lawn on a spring day as the adorable children, cuddly pets, etc., romp in the sunlight (light is a heavenly necessity). Forgotten in the rush of images, however, was her spouse of 22 years. I called this apparent omission to her attention, and she tossed it off by explaining that he would be inside watching sports or the business channel. So, one may infer that although his role as loving mate cannot be overstated, his explicit functions within the context of infinity are vague at best. One might assume that a continuation of endearing qualities such as romance, lively sex, and a sense of humor would decorate the halcyon hopes of a grateful wife.

But in heaven, as in life, a properly assigned husband may expect to be left alone until needed (as in a fourth for bridge) as a kind of social lubricant. I know lots of guys who couldn't spend two hours with their wives' relatives anyway, so for them, hell might be a more desirable option.

In subsequent forays into the hopes and aspirations of the faithful, I noted an undercurrent of sentiment typified by the following statement. "I waited on him hand and foot for forty-six years; now I have to carry him on my back for eternity?

Bring me Marco the pool boy."

"Women are meant to be loved, not to be understood."

Oscar Wilde

CYNICISM

The true cynic has only one obvious characteristic; he cannot be disappointed. This protective quality has the additional benefit of suppressing aspiration and generally tempering what most of us regard as the joy of living. Liberated from this primitive appetite, a cynic can be comfortable with his hobby of spoiling it for the rest of us, a pastime which he wryly savors.

The consequences of all his choices are in a sense the same to him. A positive outcome for anyone else can only be inadequate or unsatisfactory for him, so his disapproval will be appropriate. A negative result will be anticipated well in advance, and may best be endured in the company of others. Anything in between will be regarded as insipid and unworthy of consideration.

If heaven has a place for cynics, the gates should be guarded so none will escape into the general population. Cynicism is extremely contagious, and the most pious among us cannot long endure its potency. The gullible should be on their guard, however, since this endearing quality frequently masquerades as wit.

Since people shouldn't have to go to hell exclusively because of their opinions, it would be unfair to protect heaven by just fast-tracking them to the other place. If you can think of a group of people who would be happier in Satan's realm, I'll buy you a rosary.

Since cynicism, skepticism, pessimism and nihilism are frequently confused. I would like to offer, for the sake of perspective, the following opinions, which you may categorize according to personal interpretation.

"I don't believe in an afterlife, so I don't have to spend my whole life fearing hell, or fearing heaven even more. For whatever the tortures of hell, I think the boredom of heaven would be even worse."

Isaac Asimov

"In heaven all the interesting people are missing."

Friedrich Nietzsche

"We are our own devils: we drive ourselves out of our Edens."

Goethe

"Democracy is only a dream: it should be put in the same category as Arcadia, Santa Claus, and Heaven."

H. L. Mencken

"My childhood was a period of waiting for the moment when I could send everyone connected to it to hell."

Igor Stravinsky

"By means of shrewd lies, unremittingly repeated, it is possible to make people believe that heaven is hell---and hell heaven. The greater the lie, the more readily it will be believed."

Adolph Hitler

"Men have fiendishly conceived a heaven only to find it insipid, and a hell only to find it ridiculous."

George Santayana

"Ever notice that "what the hell" is always the right decision?"

Marilyn Monroe

If you feel unhappy or bewildered after digesting these remarks, I recommend Russian Vodka, served very, very cold.

IS THERE HUMOR IN HEAVEN?

L aughter is an earthly blessing. The effects of a merry disposition on health and longevity are well documented. So you find yourself; unwanted hand on your shoulder or forearm, flecks of spittle on your eyebrows (hopefully nowhere else), ears squinting against the unsought harsh braying in proximity, the ripe and unpleasant stench of cocktails and onion dip seeking out your nostrils, and your mind straining for liberation or at least temporary paralysis. What affliction can this be? Apparently, you are being compelled to listen to a joke.

Alas, humor is seldom a commodity to be equally shared; and art and originality are typical casualties of scripted wit. What is pleasurable in small doses may be inversely painful in larger amounts. No series of spoken words is as cloyingly irritating as an unbroken sequence of mediocre jokes delivered artlessly to a rowdy audience. You may think a Sunday sermon could rival a stand-up act for the sheer agony they can both deliver, but I'm here to stick up for the ministers of this world. At worst, the inspirational message we must endure on Sunday morning is a powerful soporific, and if your pew-mates can restrain themselves from their amens and hallelujahs, you can usually sleep off Saturday's debauch. The comedy show, however, provides a form of redundancy that even martinis can't mask. The other paying guests have a vested interest in perpetuating the rollicking zaniness, so they can foul the atmosphere with their enthusiasm as well.

Give me a Church anytime. I'll rattle the collection plate as if I'd dropped a couple of quarters in, and go back to sleep, dreaming that my piety will propel me to heaven. With any luck, the sermonizers and gagmen can entertain each other elsewhere.

"The secret source of humour itself is not joy, but sorrow. There is no humour in heaven."

Mark Twain

TWO GUYS NAMED GUS

Gustav Mahler was admitted to the Vienna Conservatoire two years before the death of Gustave Courbet in Switzerland in 1877. Mahler was fifteen and already an able and promising student of music. As his talent and reputation grew, he earned the resentment of a large percentage of the European musical establishment for his bold non-traditional interpretations. Anti-Semitism also haunted him throughout his life.

It is not uncommon for genius to flourish amid controversy and Mahler's considerable gifts were eventually acknowledged worldwide despite harsh and denigrating criticism.

Gustave Courbet enjoyed a similar reputation in the salons of Paris. He offended the pre-impressionist mood of mid-nineteenth century France with his somewhat shocking choice of subjects (nude women embracing) as well as his behavioral excesses (his love of food and drink was also well documented).

He demonstrated contempt for the opinions of his detractors and seemed to revel in the adversity he earned as well as the artistic recognition he deserved.

What, you may ask, beyond the obvious uneven but inevitable course of genius, do these two titanic influences on our culture have in common?

Courbet's long series of unsuccessful romances and estranged children leads one to assume he was not properly respectful of the fairer sex. He believed, due to his success, that he could take for granted the pleasures to which he felt entitled. (He died alone, of alcoholism). Mahler did not enjoy the company of so many women, but the most important ones were treated as inferiors. He told his wife Alma that her role was exclusively to see to his needs, and he would not tolerate her performing any creative independent function*.

If you are a male genius, and you elevate yourself beyond an entire gender, I have a nightmare for you. As you sit in the place of final judgment, and await the seating of the jury, you become vaguely aware of whispering, rustling of fabric, and lilac scent. Onto the expectant scene now files every female you have ever known; wives, mistresses, barmaids, dog-walkers, your aunt, your mother, the fat girl you teased in the eighth grade; all of them. Would your hopes be high that your mother could talk a room full of raging harpies into sparing you from the flames as the jury deliberates the various sentences? (Guilt is a foregone conclusion.)

As you listen to the screaming and violence from the adjoining chamber, you may reflect on the last time you spoke rudely to a female phone solicitor and slammed the receiver down.

When the term "fairer sex" was coined, all evidence points to the conclusion that it was a reference to complexion rather than dispassionate

---

*There may have been a glimmer of optimism for Mahler fans. He died in 1911, and as his coffin was being lowered into the earth outside Vienna, a single moment of glorious sunlight interrupted an otherwise gloomy day of torrential rain.

objectivity, so don't go around pulling any pigtails, genius or not.

"Men forget everything; women remember everything."

John Wayne

DO I BELONG HERE?

Hell must have a fair number of individuals who assume they've gotten a raw deal. Imagine every other person you encounter having palms and eyebrows upraised, demanding directions to the nearest lawyer (plenty of those in hell). Little is known about the appeals process in the lower kingdom, but interminable delays are to be expected. Catholicism used to provide a convenient temporary stopover called purgatory, where one could briefly review hell's entertainments without any permanent disfigurement, but I fear the existence of such a place may even now be in the process of reconsideration. It might be a little too easy for the partially sinful to commit grand larceny and a few misdemeanors with the only threat being a charring of the lower extremities, and then off to heaven.

I am personally uncomfortable with any spiritual expression that leaves chaos in its wake for the rest of us to sort out. The relatively modern phenomenon of suicide bombings with the expectation of paradise for the martyr (not my word) seems like a grossly distorted interpretation of anyone's religious beliefs. What sort of moral compromise must a person be capable of if as he straps on his explosives, he ignores the lives of the innocent while planning the demise of his enemies? Those who do great evil may be righteously slain in some cultures, and indiscriminate butchery should earn a just and commensurate response.

Since prejudice and bigotry would be such delicious commodities to manipulate, perhaps we could incorporate them into compartments of hell. A male suicide bomber assumes, perhaps, that he will be greeted into Paradise by comely virgins. (How happy could they be with this role, anyway?) If instead, he is welcomed by a group of leprous pornographers bent on circumcising him, he may learn regret. If you are a white racist, your hell should be populated with only fellow racists, no other white ones though. Mixing Bosnians and Serbs, Hutu and Tutsi, cowboys and Indians and any other polarized communities should work in heaven too. And if there are a few virgins left over after all the sorting, perhaps the higher-ups could work out a suitable compensation for my efforts.

"Heaven but the vision of fulfilled desire.
And Hell the Shadow from a soul on fire."
Omar Khayyan

DECEPTION

What if death is an unclear transition into the afterlife in which the unlucky decedent must guess where he has landed by the first thing he becomes aware of upon reopening his eyes?

What would you want to see? Perhaps a beloved relative or a person in monk's garb would be reassuring. It might be nice to meet a group of children (without tattoos preferably). Nuns seem to have an excellent chance for salvation, maybe in a gospel choir for atmosphere. I wouldn't be too hasty however, to take all this at face value; hell may specialize in irony.

As an example, let's say the first eyes you look into after your demise are those of a beloved terrier, a faithful and loving companion during life. You stoop to receive him as he leaps into your arms; but wait! He is snarling toward your jugular vein and your eternity would be one of vigilance against the possibility that you would be nipped to misery by a seven pound canine whom you once fed and cared for.

Hell may have many surprises for the presumptuous. My personal views may be somewhat counterintuitive. If I walked through the emptiness and encountered a room full of televangelists (grinning or crying), I would be scrambling to find another way out. I'd rather join a pair of bearded ayatollahs and play backgammon, although I speak neither Arabic nor Farsi. I'm always alert for possible hypocrisy, even in the mirror, and I particularly reject all representatives of religion who don't think that the prayers of children of any faith are heard by the same ears.

"To different minds, the same world is hell, and a heaven".

Ralph Waldo Emerson

SATAN'S OFFICE

ACT II

Satan: Can someone please find Signor Ponzi, or do I have to go digging for him myself?

Demon: Sorry chief, that division of hell is so packed with souls, we can't tell one from another.

Satan: Sooner or later humans are going to catch on, and we will have to introduce a replacement product for the pyramid scheme.

Demon: Don't be too sure. We anticipate a new wave of inductions that have inspired copycats from kindergarten on up.

Satan: All right; let's postpone that issue for a bit. Who's got something new for me?

Research Demon: Well, some of our guys secretly made a bet with a couple of

24

those feathered freaks from the other place.

Satan: I don't think I'm going to like this. What's the deal?

Research Demon: We have a few bright, greedy young suits who promise us they have designed an investment product that offers twice the risk to investors while doubling the benefits to a select few.

Satan: (Sarcastically) Daringly original! Can you be a bit more specific?

Research Demon: It's like a credit default swap. We identify huge corporations that don't actually produce anything tangible. Then we screen the entire strata of management to guarantee that a hunger for money greatly exceeds intellect or scruples.

Satan: Where will we find such a chimera?

Research Demon: Patience, chief.

Satan: Grrrr.

Research Demon: Sorry! But please hear me out. Now we locate a gullible group of well-heeled but simple-minded investors who will insure the success of our corporation against the remote possibility of collapse. Then we charge both sides a fee for introducing them to one another.

Satan: So, what's new about that?

Research Demon: The gimmick is that we simultaneously market this same opportunity at a huge discount to people who will be happy if the whole scheme collapses. The oversubscription for pennies on the dollar can be offered to North Koreans, Somali warlords, weapons dealers, fundamentalists, anarchists; anyone with an axe to grind. They either get rich or revel in economic chaos. It's a win-win for them.

Satan: I'm beginning to feel a bit tingly, but you still haven't said anything about this bet.

Research Demon: The guys we're dealing with don't want to use any of the old nomenclature. They think terms like hedge fund and credit default swap make people queasy.

Satan: And?

Research Demon:	They want to call this new package "Fucking Poison".
Satan:	(Rolls sideways off his throne.)
Research Demon:	Chief, our research tells us some people will think it's like some edgy new scent, or a Vin Diesel movie. Our guys bet that even with a name like that we can put a trillion dollars into peril within this fiscal year.
Satan:	Can people be that stupid?
Research Demon:	No stupider than angels. If we lose the bet, we're paying with worthless bonds, so it's fool-proof.
Satan:	I've heard that before.

AN ATHEIST'S VIEW

Some people live comfortably within rigid religious beliefs. Others prefer their spirituality to be interpretative and less confining. The most precise descriptions of heaven and hell, supplemented by tradition and ancestry, come from these two groups. Since I assign a high value to objectivity, I believed it my duty to consider the opinions of people who either haven't made up their minds yet, or who reject the idea of religion altogether. The fact that one system of beliefs is much more popular than another does not validate it. Popularity is a feeble criterion for truth.

Admittedly, coaxing a response (to questions about an afterlife) other than a knowing smirk from a confirmed atheist can be discouraging. It was necessary to create analogies like right and wrong for God and Satan, good and evil for heaven and hell, etc. With enough flexibility, and sufficient alcohol to lubricate the imagination, I was able to obtain some useful notions. My overall impression of the theists who shared their ideas with me is that they are grateful for the comfort and structure of religion. Atheists seemed no less comfortable with justice and propriety outside of the umbrella of faith. It did not occur to me that sinful behavior would be exclusive to either group.

I prompted an unbelieving, but very intelligent and attractive friend to contrive a hypothetical eternity. Her life, given her natural advantages, must be so rewarding that heaven would be at best a step sideways or slightly down, and the gross imbalance of a hell unthinkable. In fairness to her objectivity, she distributes her contempt equally among all supernatural beliefs. Buddhism, Gomarism, Catholicism, Gnosticism and all the countless other hopes of the restlessly faithful are treated equally. Not that she is openly disrespectful; she is convinced that in the absence of organized religion, too many directionless individuals would be caroming randomly about like pinballs, making life inconvenient for the rest of us.

I conceded that point but pressed on for a specific response to the heaven-hell fiction (her term). She suggested (quite reasonably I thought) that we begin with hell and work upwards. Since her ideal existence has justice and fairness (not Karma !) as a foundation, she proposed that those qualities should be present in any sensible afterlife. Importantly, she opined, scale and proportionality should also carry through eternally, thus doubly damning those whose misdeeds affect large numbers of people. History has provided a Pandora's Box of despots, embezzlers, politicians, unlicensed surgeons, lawyers, lobbyists, and cultists etc. who will keep emerging into the daylight to earn our collective revulsion.

At this point, she paused reflectively and declared that the first candidates to populate her hypothetical hell should be George (you know which one) Bush and Dick Cheney, as if somehow their presence would transform any place to a kind of hell. Now, just a darn minute, I said. Many may as-

sume that Mr. Cheney is a "porcus ex grege di-
aboli"*, but George W. Bush may belong elsewhere. I
earnestly believe that he is not a bad, bad, bad man.
He may be morally ambiguous and a bit dishonest
but his charming naiveté is hardly evil.

Old Catholicism had a place for unbaptized in-
fants and those too mentally challenged to know
right from wrong called limbo (also a dance with a
stick). If new Catholicism hadn't tossed limbo out
with Saint Christopher, GWB might have more options.

Even though her hell consisted of only two individuals, she seemed impatient to move on with the
interview. I prepared myself for some interesting fiction flavored with sarcasm, but this was not her
heaven. Instead, she asked me what I knew about
"the beast with two backs"†. With what I took to be a
needlessly provocative gesture, she indicated that I
could find her heaven there. This concept may lend
itself to additional research so I concluded the interview.

*"Heaven is an item from the cave of the thief of
dreams."*

Ilachem

*"When I die I hope I go to Heaven, whatever the
Hell that is."*

Ayn Rand

---

*Swine from the devil's herd. (With thanks to George M. Fraser
and his knowledge of the classics.)
†Coitus

THE REWARDS OF SCIENCE

Have you wondered how the lives of Stephen Hawking or Joe DiMaggio would have turned out if they had been around 500 years ago? The likelihood of their respective successes in iron mongering or game keeping seems tenuous to nullity, but we shall never know. Much of the distinction we may earn in our seventy-odd years may be directly attributable to the era into which we were born.

Consider the unfortunate circumstances of the life of Giordano Bruno. He was lucky enough to be born into a prosperous family that could afford to educate him in a traditional, religious style. He also enjoyed the advantage of a versatile and intuitive nature, as well as a powerful intellect, which precipitated the inevitable departure from tradition that was to doom him. Bruno ran afoul of the Catholic Church by persistently and vocally making claims that seemed to argue for the existence of an infinite universe. Infinity was the exclusive property of God in the sixteenth century, and the idea of contradiction to an Italian cardinal was as accelerant to a flame.

If he had arrived on the scene 200 years earlier or later, he may have been spared the warmest kind of death, but by his stubborn refusal to abandon his originality, he was compelled to become one with the fire. Thus, his ultimate arrival in heaven or hell (totally unclear) was no doubt accompanied by the smell of scorched sandals.

Science and religion have historically been compelled to endure an adversarial relationship. Long before Galileo's inconvenient (heretical?) clashes with Pope Urban VIII over the nature of the universe, organized religion has had to cope with the distracting and erosive influence of science.

I arbitrarily chose the sixteenth century as the genesis of challenges of the most significant scientific matters that had long been part of the foundations of Christianity, however, scientific historians might push that time frame back a century or two.

Before that, one pictures the odd friar, railing away at alchemists or astrologists or practitioners of any so-called science with the prefix "trans" in it, but with a somewhat farcical tone.

We of the twenty-first century take these issues more seriously, as is detectable in our representative form of government; not that plenty of politicians aren't gifted comedians.

Modern man debates evolution, stem cell research, and birth control, to name a few points of controversy.

Where church and science diverge, the fork in the road to heaven or hell may be defined. Faith was once an unquestioning commitment to the reality of beliefs for which there is no physical evidence. Since modern scientific techniques regarding the determination of the age of the universe and the mechanics of evolution are so persuasive, they fly in the face of religious doctrine. The faithful must now actively reject increasingly powerful evidence that contradicts biblical interpretations. The requisites of faith are more demanding than ever before, and so, I presume are the criteria involved in the selection process for the afterlife.

An excess of information gleaned from empirical exercises such as scientific testing might handicap an aspirant for everlasting peace.

If you are sufficiently motivated to search for the path to a traditional heaven, I offer the following useful list of things to avoid, and their attendant perils.

1. Cosmetic surgery: Few medical practices rival this insult to celestial design. If you are born with too many legs, learn to play soccer.
2. Genetically enhanced food crops: You better say grace before you eat this stuff. I hear it tastes the same, but the devil's fingerprints are all over it. It might not be sinful to ship this commodity to the godless starving multitudes however, so don't sell your biotech stock yet.
3. Molecular research: There's just too much temptation here. People will be placing flecks of gold in rodent ova with hopes of raising golden rats. If it's smaller than an animalcule, don't touch it !
4. Astrophysics: If you have spent time reflecting on the nature of terms like parsec and event horizon, or if you are intellectually encumbered by numbers with high exponential values, then you haven't spent enough time with the Scriptures.
5. Science Fiction: As if science, per se, were not inherently troublesome enough, toss a little fiction in with it and you can imagine the most egregious distortions. Embellishing simple biological forms with grotesque qualities

from the imaginations of human deviants is likely to confuse even the most guarded mind.

"The poet only asks to get his head into the heavens. It is the logician who seeks to get the heavens into his head. And it is his head that splits."
G. K. Chesterton (1874-1936), Orthodoxy

AD INFERNO TECUM
"GO TO HELL"

Wishing someone into eternal torment is a sentiment no religion I am aware of sanctions. People say it all the time, but I doubt that is often intended in a literal way. In fact, from my observations, the anger that once begot that simple curse has transformed itself into a need to humiliate some unlucky soul into an unwanted sex act. The hard consonants of a phrase like "go get fucked" suit the mood of an angry cabbie or the recipient of an unsolicited sales call in a way that attaches passion to simple impatience. Fortunately for the user, he has uttered neither curse nor blasphemy, thus committed no sin.

Excessive profanity, or vulgarity if you prefer, may be considered misdemeanors in some places, so be cautious about venting indiscreetly.

Sending someone to hell would be a cute trick, but I don't think any pope or saint could get authorization, and if it were possible, people would be winking out of existence at a fearful rate and we would notice.

Whenever I am feeling anger toward my girlfriend for mistreating or humiliating me (her hobbies), I picture the sand-worms from the science fiction classic "Dune" rising up to swallow her and return

her to her Dark Master. It's not that I would condemn her forever to the fires of hell; I would simply
like to see some of the rough edges singed off. I'm
pretty sure that after a semester or two of torture
and screaming, (not hers) Satan would toss her
back as too harsh for the environment. She has a
loving side, as you might expect, but it is like the
flavorful but mild Mahi; incomplete unless flavored
by the peppery toxins from a Cajun kitchen. Her
time in hell would be spent reminding people to
keep toilet seats down and separate whites from colors in the laundry. Trivial, you may believe, but no
earthly cause has been pursued more intensely than
my little cloven hoofed mate's quest for sequential,
methodical, geometric, paralyzing, universal order.
To that end, her enthusiasm and volume will exceed
any of history or literature's best known harridans,
and she is not, I repeat not tempted by compromise.

(This chapter had to be written totally in her absence for obvious reasons.)

"Divorces are made in heaven."
                                    Oscar Wilde (1854-1900)

SATAN'S OFFICE

ACT III

Satan:
Has anyone else noticed how slippery the floors are getting?

Demon (reluctantly):
I think it has something to do with the last thirty years' harvest.

Satan:
What the hell's that supposed to mean?

Demon:
You see chief, as standards of living went up, prosperity brought obesity; then we get 'em.

Satan:
So this oily film that's on the floor is really....

Demon:
Yep. As soon as the flames hit them, the adipose tissue starts turning into a greasy vapor that coats everything. We had an eight year old American boy

	that weighed almost six hundred pounds come in the other day.
Satan:	Astonishing!
Demon:	We had to boil him for two days before we could throw him into the fire. It's exhausting our resources and taking up too much space.
Satan:	Don't we get skinny people anymore?
Demon:	Those people have neither the inclination nor the strength to commit a decent sin chief, so they mostly go to the other place.
Satan:	Well I won't have this place smelling like a truck stop diner. Start freezing them until we build a gravy factory or get into the bio-fuel business.
Demon:	Roger, chief.

THE BLESSING OF WORDS

Some brief consideration should be given to the importance of language in the afterlife. The joy and impact of words on our brief lives cannot be underestimated, thus it seems some notions of heaven must include the ability to communicate. Isolation from the influence of others seems more a tool of hell. Anyone doubting the potency of the medium should be aware that the wrong words typed onto a computer can send you to jail and into the hands of some athletic individuals who will teach you the sport of water-boarding. Conversely, the right words can pave the road to the Presidency of the United States. These words may have no hint of veracity, but they should be used by a person who can successfully simulate sincerity. So if words can turn a cockroach into a prince, let's make a place for them in eternity.

Not all words or combinations thereof will be welcome in a sensible heaven; for instance, vertiginous, flatulence, and puke should be unnecessary since the unpleasantness they all evoke will be nonexistent. Short but useful words like God, hail, love, olé, groovy, and amen should be enough to accommodate all but the longwinded. Even punctuation marks merit re-evaluation. The double and triple exclamation point will be more frequently used, and the question mark can be disposed of altogether (parentheses are in limbo). Don't suppose you won't hear plenty of Latin in heaven. "Cogito, ergo sum" is a testimony to the individuality we shall want to take to heaven with us. We will not have to use the words woe or sin unless we're gossiping about the southern neighbors, nor will redundancy be tolerated.

All forms of over-usage and misappropriation will be relegated to what is truly, I believe, a kind of linguistic hell. The following phrases would be the exclusive currency of the damned:

a) It is what it is. (Fittingly final)
b) Been there, done that. (Boredom can be hellish)
c) Awesome! (The first word that comes out of your mouth as you behold the eternal fire)

There should be a probationary review for the sin of being unoriginal in the higher estates. It's a shame all words don't carry the same weight as the monosyllabic goliath pi (or π).

If someone knows a symbol or word that has more information in it than that one, I'd like to know about it. It is so elegantly reductive that it has been etched into a heat-resistant slab and shot into space so our extra-terrestrial neighbors can better understand us.

"I am not so lost in lexicography as to forget that words are the daughters of earth and that things are the sons of heaven."

Dr. Samuel Johnson

MURRAY'S NIGHT CLUB HEAVEN

In order to fully appreciate the blissful nature of a nightclub heaven, it might be necessary for the reader to temporarily suspend his doubts regarding the role of sexuality in the afterlife.

Suggestive dancing and the casual use of alcohol may also cause queasiness among the temperate, although heaven's intoxicants are unlikely to have any secondary consequences. Consider the line of hopefuls at heaven's gate; patiently awaiting Saint Peter, who is nattily clad in pimpy urban chic, checking credentials and passing the most beautiful without undue scrutiny. The most observant among them will note the vibration in the vertical bars of the gate in response to the robust bass emanating from within.

This place seems pretty hip.

As Murray steps inside, (media pass) he happily notes the easygoing, good-natured mingling that permeates the atmosphere. The lighting is subdued but adequate, except near the band and dance floor naturally, and the entire vignette is now animated by a driving Latin beat. The service staff are comely, slender, and models of hygiene, and the restrooms are clean enough for elective surgery. Pleasantly fortified by his first cocktail, he approaches someone to dance.

Murray:	Excuse me, would you like to dance?
She:	I was just thinking about asking you the same question, but would you mind if my friend joins us? I don't want to leave her alone.
Dance floor:	Step, step, slide, writhe, undulate. (We quickly adjust to each other's rhythm and the three of us move temptingly close with only the lightest of touches).
Them:	(afterwards) Thanks that was great.
Murray:	Pant, gasp.

(Note the absence of the unnecessary tedium of questions regarding age, employment, or mutual acquaintance. This sort of chatter is puerile and unimaginative, therefore unworthy of heaven.)

She:	I'm Chelsea, and this is Madonna.
Murray:	Pant, gasp, mumble.
Madonna:	What's your name?
Murray:	M-m-murray. (I'm beginning to bring my heart rate down). How about three shots of Tequila?

| Them: | (They just look at each other and smirk knowingly). |

The events that comprise the next few hours (?) are familiar to all of us. There is excessive flattery, lots of laughter, more dancing, exaggeration and hyperbole, fueled by multiple stimuli etc, etc. It is ritualized, but it never goes out of style. Random strangers wander briefly into this amiable circle, but their functions are exclusively as bit players. Finally, the girls decide to leave.

| Chelsea: | Murray, could you escort us to the car? |

| Murray: | I am pleased to serve. |

| Chelsea: | (Outside) Can Madonna help you find your keys (Does this mean her hands will be in my pockets?) while I whisper a few temptations in your ear, or would you prefer she stay in the car? |

| Murray: | B-but I haven't paid my bar tab. (If you are sensitive enough to care about giving offense by refusing a lovely invitation, then you will be familiar with the old "bar tab" dodge.) |

| Chelsea: | Well here's my address. Go back and have some fun, (see if you can improve on me/us) and I'll make you an omelet later. |

We part.

I tried to contrive a heaven that wouldn't have any obvious sinning in it, but you may have noted a phrase or two with a slightly titillating tone. If you say two Hail Marys, I think your conscience should be relieved.

"You have to forget about what other people say; when you're suppose to die, when you're suppose to be lovin'. You have to forget about all these things. You have to go on and be crazy. Craziness is like heaven.

Jimi Hendrix (1942-1970)

CLUB HELL

Compared to Club Heaven, this place seems pretty easy to get into; No dress code, no health code, no cover charge, no line of hopefuls. I've traveled a great distance, though, so I'm going in. The first thing I notice is the heavy pall of tobacco smoke that induces a fat man to cough so hard that a handgun falls out of his coat pocket. No bartender takes note of my arrival, so I remain hot and thirsty, but the music isn't bad (Metallica, I think). There is a separate part of the room where drooling, libidinous men are encouraging what I believe to be a human female to dance with a shiny pole. I'm beginning to have misgivings.

A bombshell in a cocktail waitress getup asks me if I would like a drink, so I order to be polite. As I tip her, she leans forward to kiss me (a grateful, not a passionate kiss I thought). Her lips seize mine, and then her teeth dig into my flesh, and I flinch and taste my blood as it flows between us. My screams are drowned out by the music, but I finally pull away, noticing for the first time the shadow of a moustache and the hint of an Adam's apple that my assailant sports under my caking gore.

I look around anxiously, hoping to find some kindred soul with whom to share some trivial common interest at least, but I'm not optimistic. Wait a minute! There's my old high school gym coach talking to a state legislator I vaguely recognize. They share a booth with a guy in religious headgear and a man in a military uniform. Holy shit, its Idi Amin, and his eyes are glowing bright red!

I'm taking my car with anything the valet forgot to steal and getting the hell out of here.

"Hell is other people".

Jean-Paul Sartre

FOUR SHORT BIOGRAPHIES

The following four chapters have a common theme, and could have been integrated into a single essay, but the characters have left such a momentous impact on their time as to entitle them to elaboration.

What Tomás de Torquemada, Feng-Shan Ho, Raoul Wallenberg and Pope Pius XII have in common is a historical and startling interface with generations of Jews. Heaven and hell must be alerted well in advance of the arrival of luminaries such as these, and when souls in large numbers take flight like great flocks of birds on the rise, a few moments of inconsistent morality may be more definitive than decades of prayer.

"Do not ask God the way to heaven; he will show you the hardest one."

Stanislaw J. Lee (1909 - 1966)

"The hottest places in Hell are reserved for those who in time of great moral crises maintain their neutrality."

Dante Alighieri

THE GRAND INQUISITOR

If you were challenged to name a Christian clergy-man whose morality may be justly doubted, what name jumps to mind? Do you think of decadent French Popes, pedophiles, or perhaps Jonestown? There is a delicious variety of rogues whose apparent hypocrisy renders them eligible for condemnation, but Tomás de Torquemada has established his reputation not only as an individual but as a symbol of a move-ment.

The exposure and elimination of heresy was the obsession of the Christian hierarchy in Spain during the second half of the fifteenth century. The Inquisi-tion did not exclusively target Jews. The focus of the majority of its inquiries was to identify those Jews and Muslims who, though converted to Catholicism, practiced the rituals of other faiths in private.

Since Spain had the largest population of con-verted Jews in Europe, the timing and incentive for a cleansing was ideal. Ferdinand and Isabella, to whom Torquemada was confessor, are generally re-membered for their sponsorship of Christopher Columbus' adventures, not for their support of a cruel and murderous purge.

In my twelve years of Catholic education, I can't recall any information that impugned the reputation of Isabella, nor were the excesses of the Inquisition too closely examined.

It turns out that if you wanted to save the soul of a nominal heretic (likely a Jew), it was perfectly reasonable to torture him into acquiescence. The notorious auto-da-fé (act of faith) allowed the interviewee the unattractive choices of death before being burned (for those who recanted and kissed the cross before being mounted upon it), death in the fire with quick-burning wood (for those who merely recanted), and death over slow-burning wood (for those who refused to recant). As public spectacles go, hangings and beheadings couldn't compete with the auto-da-fé. Not only does the constriction of the throat or removal of the head deprive the witness of the stimuli of prolonged and desperate screaming, the fire enlarges the theatricality of the affair in a symbolically incomparable way. Did people really watch this without revulsion, or am I naïve about the proper oversight of St. Peter's flock?

Whether Torquemada executed his grim task out of a sense of duty, or whether there was some scintilla of pleasure to tantalize him, we shall never know, unless we join him somewhere perhaps.

We do know that his lively tenure as Grand Inquisitor was accompanied by a persistent fear for his personal safety. He rarely traveled without a large armed escort and he worried obsessively about the introduction of poison into his meals. Oh yes, he had one other teensy issue; his grandmother was a converted Jew. On the plus side, he was considered an incorruptible and zealous defender of the faith.

Would a simple confession deprive Satan of a paranoid monk who was said to have the horn of a unicorn beside his bed as an antidote to frustrate poisoners?

"I hold it the inalienable right of anybody to go to hell in his own way."

Robert Frost

PIUS XII

If you chose to write a biography based purely on the volume of information extant, you could do worse than select a Pope. The problem is that the Vatican metes out information as it sees fit, which is most frequently biased toward the positive image of the Catholic church, so it will be somewhat idealized, like a portrait on a coin.

Once a Pope is elected, his life is carefully arranged to conform to customs and restrictions that are centuries old, so don't expect to see a Pope on a skateboard or at Starbuck's.

Pius XII, like all his predecessors, was compelled to live in an environment in which his daily activities and comments, meetings, recreations, etc. were duly recorded by the meticulous Vatican scribes. If a Pope wanted to test the acoustics of the Sistine Chapel by farting in various parts of the room, it would be recorded and sketched for preservation in the vast archives.

Pius has been considered seriously for canonization to sainthood for decades. The obstacle to this comes oddly not from within the Church itself, but from a few pesky Jewish historians. Apparently, the Pope's behavior prior to and during World War II was somewhat more passive than those who appreciate the preservation of Jewish lives would have had it. When he was a cardinal, his role as diplomat brought him into close contact with a number of questionable Germans.

Although he is on record as protesting Nazi violations of the Reichskonkordat (an unenforceable political document between the Vatican and Germany), his opposition was not sufficiently vigorous to satisfy his detractors. Those who condemn him accuse him of badly timed indifference during crisis. His defenders suggest that he was only able to intercede on behalf of the persecuted by acting under the radar, as it were, with subtlety and discretion.

Pope Benedict XVI (can you name another German Pope?) has generously put the canonization process on hold for a bit in deference to those skeptics, but you'll have to hold your breath for quite a while if you think this can all be clarified with additional evidence from the Vatican. The archivist in charge says it will be six or seven years before the requested material can be found, sorted, and provided. How many holocaust survivors will be alive when that curtain is raised?

If Saints and Popes don't qualify for immediate entry into heaven, what chance do the rest of us have? If Pius XII has ascended, perhaps he has a phalanx of robed confessors to fend off the non-Christians with too many questions who may have strayed into that part of heaven.

"I desire to go to Hell not to Heaven. In Hell I shall enjoy the company of popes, kings and and princes, but in Heaven are only beggars, monks, hermits and apostles."

Niccoló Machiavelli

HO

The fiction that Austria's 200,000 Jews might escape the persecution that was already evident in Germany was shattered in 1938 after the "Kristallnacht". While that perceived threat inspired callous indifference in some non-Jews, others sought bravely, if vainly to oppose the Nazi machine. A very few individuals were in a position to actually make a difference, specifically foreign diplomats, who were at least temporarily able to act outside Germany's oppressive influence.

If you thought you had to be a white Christian to save Jews, let me introduce you to Feng-Shan Ho. Considered "China's Schindler", he may have been responsible for saving thousands of Viennese Jews before 1940. As first Secretary of the Chinese legation, he was, against the orders of his superiors, able to issue visas to Shanghai which enabled their holders to safely emigrate.

Although the early colonial powers zealously tried to bring the word of the Christian God to the East, Buddhism and Shinto, among other practices, prevailed. So can really good Buddhists reach our unfamiliar heaven? Of course! They may not like it at first, but the eternal bliss should be an irresistible opiate. St. Peter is not expected to sort according to color or height.

"To be able to practice five things everywhere under heaven constitutes perfect virtue...gravity, generosity of soul, sincerity, earnestness, and kindness. "

Confucius (551 BC – 479 BC)

RAOUL

The most admirable qualities may be forged in the crucible of human tragedy. Once again the horrors of Nazi Germany framed the remarkable life of a man who realized the importance of his own existence in time to change misery to salvation for others.

Raoul Wallenberg's story is one of heroism and mystery. Picture a handsome Swedish diplomat, running on the top of a moving freight car full of Jews, slipping protective documents into the desperate hands of the condemned. Witnesses suggest that German riflemen deliberately aimed high out of admiration for this act of bravery. The life that Wallenberg once lived, as a businessman, then a diplomat, was abandoned so he could give his full energy to saving as many of Budapest's Jews as possible. He bartered, cajoled, and bullied his way through negotiations with Nazi officials who learned to respect him for his dogged advocacy.

Although personally responsible for saving countless lives, he was apparently unable to save his own. Did the Nazis finally get him? Did God just say well done, and vacuum him right out of Hungary and into heaven? No one knows for sure, but there is evidence that a brutal and poorly managed Russian army of occupation might be to blame. He just left with his chauffeur one day and vanished.

His destination was the Russian military headquarters at Debrecen, but the occupiers have offered few clues as to what may have happened to him there, if he even arrived. The claim that Wallenberg died in a Soviet prison on July 17, 1947 is considered suspect by most historians, but little other information about his fate is available. Ladies and gentlemen, what of his immortal soul? Heaven! Case closed.

"The brightest crowns that are worn in heaven have been tried, and smelted, and polished, and glorified through the furnace of tribulation."

Edward Chapin

SATAN'S OFFICE

ACT IV

Demon:　　　　We got some trouble with new arrivals chief.

Satan:　　　　What now?

Demon:　　　　There's a group of new suicide bombers who were delivered at the same time as a batch of lawyers.

Satan:　　　　Don't tell me you let them talk to each other.

Demon:　　　　It was an accident chief. They just seemed to have a mutual affinity. Before we could do anything to discourage them, the lawyers were bleating about breach of contract and demanding virgins for their new clients.

Satan:	Demanding? Ridiculous. Where would we find virgins anyway?
Demon:	We've got three from the sixteenth century, but they're so mean, we pretty much leave them alone.
Satan:	Can't we just incinerate the lot of them in the waiting area?
Demon:	We got rules chief.
Satan:	So put veils on the lawyers so the bombers can't tell they're facing the other direction. Then, tell them that's the only kind of virgin available.
Demon:	But chief, they're lawyers. They've probably got no virgin parts left.
Satan:	Let 'em try to prove that in court.

INTEGRATION

Since you might hope to carry some part of your identity into the next life, other folks will probably feel the same way. Given the opportunity, we would all preserve what we consider our most admirable traits and package them into a version of ourselves no one else could recognize.

The heaven we aspire to might be distorted by similar incongruities. Imagine yourself, a virtual paragon, surrounded by treasured family, friends, and beloved pets. Uncle Woody is there without his cane, without his distinctively tobacco-flavored breath, and without the interminable stories of his youth in Ohio. He could bore a dog to sleep, even if he were simultaneously scratching him above the tail. Your grandma would be there, only without the fresh-baked cookie smell and the comfortable shoes. She would have perky breasts, bright lipstick, and the salacious smile that drove the village swains wild as she bent over the milking stool.

Since many distinctively human qualities like warts and underarm hair will be absent, how will we know one another? All friends and family will be like Teflon simulacra. Even the pets may lose their individuality. They can be surgically, if not genetically engineered like odorless dogs or hypoallergenic cats to fit into their new surroundings.

This rosy picture can only apply if heaven is highly compartmentalized. Intruders from other strata might clash for any number of reasons. Since most of our collective experiences are within a twentieth or twenty-first century context, we moderns will be ill-prepared to deal with the residents who may have preceded us by thousands of years. There is evidence of controlled fire, which anthropologists believe is a sure sign of humanity, from more than 50,000 years ago. The ignorance of the primitives, however, should not preclude their access to opportunities like heaven.

The gossamer tier of paradise that we will occupy may be overrun by knuckle-dragging, mouth-breathing, foul smelling, excessively hirsute anthropoids (and I'm just talking about the females) who were kind and just in life. We have no control over that velvet rope, so don't expect the character of the gentry to conform to your naïve preferences. That barking you hear outside might not be your golden retriever; it might be the neighbors making love.

"Somewhere, and I can't find where, I read about an Eskimo hunter who asked the local missionary priest, "If I did not know about God and sin, would I go to hell?" "No", said the priest, "not if you did not know." "Then why" asked the Eskimo earnestly, "did you tell me?"

Annie Dillard

AMBITION

Skyscrapers, fortunes, railroads and pyramids may fool their creators into a presumed intimacy with immortality. This legacy business probably doesn't extend much beyond whatever bed or race car you're lying in when you die however.

Let's assume some guy approaches the moment of judgment with a résumé that includes four theme-oriented Las Vegas Casinos and a race track. Another boasts of a single incident wherein he fed a stray cat. I'll lay eight to five on the cat lover to prevail if there's only one place left.

Some people string charitable events together in their lives with hardly a moment of hesitation. I'm afraid I might be calling the newspapers to make sure my philanthropy would not be ignored by the IRS. If I had a billion dollars or a pyramid, perhaps I'd adjust my sense of values, but as of this moment, I am fashionably unimpressed with the material world. I am moved by the beauty of aspiration, and I hope that I can elevate myself to the standards I have imposed on others.

"The pride of dying rich raises the loudest laugh in hell."

John Foster

"How you behave toward cats here below determines your status in heaven."

Robert A. Heinlein

REDUNDANCY

I know you've heard this before, but does redundancy make you frantic and ill-tempered? When you hear a cell phone tone for the eighty-sixth time, does your adrenal gland start throbbing? How about the word "awesome"? Do you wish as fervently as I do for those two syllables to fade from common usage? If the devil is in the detail, he is hard at work thinking about things that torture us on earth that he can adapt to suit hell's purposes.

Picture yourself in an unfurnished prison cell with no human contact and no object other than a small rock to keep you company. Imagine further, your favorite song recorded by Bea Arthur and played day after day, hour upon hour. How long before you would try to use the rock to give yourself the concussion that would deafen you? Let's enhance the vignette by adding a normal domestic cat which walks by the cell once a day without acknowledging you. If you couldn't do anything to impair your hearing with the rock, how long would it be before you started looking at the rock when the cat walked by and think about venting your frustration upon the innocent animal?

Redundancy is not fast-acting like cyanide, but it can make you believe there are fates worse than death. The heavy-handed example I used doesn't mean that much less malignant forms of repetition wouldn't drive a healthy person into depression and worse. I am told it is possible to laugh, hiccup, or itch yourself to death, but fortunately, the human heart generally fails before the hapless victim is driven irretrievably mad with the anticipation of the next spasm. Hell may be comprised of the simplest, most energy-efficient ways of dealing with the damned.

There are three notable exceptions to the redundancy rule. Would you guess kittens, prayers, or marijuana? Absolutely not! Not necessarily in order of their importance, they are compliments, orgasms, and chocolate milkshakes. If any of these items turn up in hell, I would be surprised. I offer a word of caution, however. All three of these treasures are frequently and easily counterfeited, and their shelf life is limited, so beware of imitations.

"The mind is its own place, and in itself, can make heaven of Hell, and a hell of Heaven."

John Milton

THE RAPTURE
(THE CHRISTIAN TERMINUS)

The most sophisticated setting to which I have ever been exposed was the home of a delightful pair of retired academics. The comfortable but elegant furnishings, especially the bookcase, with its beautifully bound treasures, provided evidence suggesting a life well lived. There was even a pair of Modigliani (heaven, I hope) portraits which understatedly bracketed an antique dictionary stand. I didn't even know there was so specialized an item. A Tiffany style lamp yielded its soft light on an opened O.E.D., which, given the geometry of the setting, was the central element of the configuration. Words and their meanings must have been very important to the happiness of this aristocratic pair.

Some words, due to ambiguity or vagueness, deserve extra attention. I feel I have a sense of the contemporary notion of rapture, but it clearly represents an idea with many individual interpretations. O.E.D.'s number five definition is "Transport of mind, ecstasy; ecstatic delight or joy". If you're curious about definition number one, it's "The act of seizing and carrying off as prey or plunder." The English language is playfully sprinkled with nuance and humor.

Anyway, as for meaning number 5, I have a difficult time obstructing the visual image of rooms full of white folks with arms raised and eyes closed, swaying to some inner message. If we're talking about ecstasy, most adolescents would think of loud music and promiscuity, helped along by abuse of a dangerously intoxicating little pill. This disparity doesn't help with the dilemma of matching the word rapture to any identifiable hope.

If I am deserving of salvation, will I be immersed in some kind of sensory bouillabaisse?? Will there by any memory of visual, tactile, auditory, or olfactory stimuli? I don't know how long the pleasing sensation of goose bumps could be endurable. So far, no image I can contrive compares to life on earth with all its shortcomings. This, of course, plausibly implies that I am a creature with many thoughts but few good ideas. Faith is the belief that things can be even better than you can imagine them. The rapture may represent a limitless expression of that ideal, but I'd like to try a little taste before I sign the contract.

"Ah, but a man's reach should exceed his grasp – or what's a heaven for?"
Robert Browning (1812-1889)

MOM

During the course of the creation of these essays and interviews, my mother inadvertently produced the raw material for this one by becoming ill enough to scare the family. If she recovers, she will certainly be amused by these premature observations. If she does not, and can look down from the heaven to which all 90 year old Catholic women will go*, she will be amused. It is not my intention to trivialize this mutual experience by relating it, although its inclusion among some of the more childish chapters of this book may seem irreverent.

I study the strain in her eyes as she attempts to articulate a single simple idea, and I know I am witnessing the continuing death of the brain cells that sculpted a strong and lovable personality.

My experience is not unique, but that is cold comfort. Every moment that you watch someone close to you suffer seems so much longer, permitting you to reflect thoroughly on whether a hasty death might be more merciful. During the times that she rests comfortably with her eyes closed, I try to contrive my most soothing tone and subject matter and ramble on stupidly.

---

*What kind of sin would a 90 year old woman be capable of?

A decade ago, she would have driven me from the room for precipitating boredom of this magnitude, but she doesn't object, so I continue.

Most mammals obey the instinct to curl up and die when the moment is right. Creatures whose hearts beat faster can expire even more efficiently; but we, as a species, understandably protract death. The best and worst medical practices have been responsible for extending life, and thus suffering, for longer than nature might have designed. Who is to say?

Hell's inmates might disagree, but I cannot easily imagine pain greater than watching someone you love suffer. Aren't there a large number of people, parents of terminally ill children for example, who would willingly sacrifice themselves to any fate if a loved one could be spared? Spiritually, it seems like a win-win situation. The unfortunate victim would be propelled to his reward on the cushion of love that pours from the hearts of his selfless and deserving sympathizers. I don't know if I'd jump directly into hell for mom, but that's the kind of idea that pops into your head along with matricide and potential funeral expenses. (She would surely find that witty).

However this ordeal evolves, I have learned to contort my mouth into a hopefully reassuring but grotesque smile when every other part of me is crying. That talent may be useful somewhere down the road.

"Heaven and earth have no pity. They regard all things as straw dogs."

Lao-Tzu

As of this printing, mom has returned home and is enjoying the benefits and challenges of rehabilitation.

GUILT

The pivotal role played by guilt in the disposition of souls should not be underestimated. It will accompany most of us from cradle to grave and far beyond, outliving qualities many would deem more endearing. Guilt, in its many manifestations, sculpts our trivial happy natures into the grim monoliths that are necessary to survive a life of atonement for sins, both real and imagined. If your personality is not properly annealed by guilt, you will be unlikely to cope with the pretense necessary to enjoy family gatherings (particularly with in-laws) for example.

Guilt, simply stated, helps us relate our every act to our base natures and gives us the strength to produce a deceptive and artificial façade to compensate. If you are able to smile and say "I'd love to" when your stomach is flexing to expel its contents, then you have begun to cultivate a symbiotic relationship with your most constant companion.

All that is to the good. The charming and decorative personality trait I have described is not the same thing you take to hell with you. **That** guilt is the exclusive property of the damned. It is not a mere twinge of the conscience; it is a growing stain on your spiritual identity, and whether or not it is acknowledged, it will expand. It is this badge that you will wear as you are introduced to Beelzebub and his friends, and it will be valid for eternity. So here's my advice for managing this ubiquitous commodity skillfully. Guilt offers splendid leverage for influencing your own behavior or that of those closest to you, but be certain you've shed most of it before you expire, because it's like taking gasoline to a fireworks display.

"The Baptists believe in The Right to Life before you're born. They also believe in Life After Death, but that is a privilege and you have to earn it by spending the interim in guilt-ridden misery. At an early age I decided that living a life of pious misery in the hope of going to heaven when it's over is a lot like keeping your eyes shut all through a movie in the hope of getting your money back in the end."

A. Whitney Brown, "The Big Picture"

BEETHEAVEN

Since it cannot be accurately imagined, there should be no restrictions on designing one's eternity to conform to preferences. Contriving a heaven for those most deserving for instance, seems like a conceit that would be both challenging and amusing. What you create, however, could be so ambiguous as to discourage the most meticulous engineer. Even a patient God would snicker at a puny effort like the following example.

Ludwig Von Beethoven, by virtue of his extraordinary gifts and reverberating impact on millions of grateful music lovers, should be a candidate for eternal bliss. His résumé seems enhanced by the irony of an affliction that progressively deafened him during what were arguably his most creative years. So I, as the architect of this particular afterlife, introduce a somewhat confused Ludwig into a room with vaulted, acoustically ideal ceilings and a perfectly positioned concert grand piano. Sitting poised over this magnificent instrument is an individual with craggily handsome features, long flowing hair, and remarkable hands*. He is, of course, Franz Liszt; not only a

---

*Although Liszt has long been known for his singular hands, it was not their actual size that was special. His fingers were not confined by typical anatomical webbing, thus the span of his hands was somewhat greater than normal.

composer of considerable genius, but a brilliant performer. His concerts were characterized by an enthusiasm that frequently left audiences breathless. His fortissimo was so vigorous that even Beethoven might enjoy him. Hell, Munich might enjoy him if he were playing in Vienna. The skeptical reader may now be uncomfortable with a growing awareness of anachronism or other inconsistency, such as "If this is heaven, why can't Beethoven just regain his hearing?"

Perhaps my (remember I'm the designer of this particular heaven) notion of bliss is the first sip of water after a long thirst, not a kidney-shaped swimming pool. Moreover, a believable heaven cannot be restricted by time or logic.

Anyway, Ludwig, awed by the performance of his 9th symphony by Master Franz, begins to weep gratefully and uncontrollably. If heaven were simplicity, perhaps the chapter should end at this point, but my heaven is made of gaudier stuff. Let's put someone at the window, witnessing this singular event. It seems to be Salieri, who is also in tears, but his tears may spring from envy (recall his supposed relationship with Mozart). Wolfgang himself is beside his old mentor, scribbling manically in a notebook as he is inspired by the auditory feast, too consumed to notice all the crying. I briefly considered the addition of Ansel Adams flitting around capturing the whole affair with his favorite instrument, the mini-cam laser recorder, but a sense of artistic hesitation thwarted this impulse. You see, sometimes you can shoot for *ad infinitum* (apropos to the general topic) and hit *ad nauseam*.

Since I was raised Catholic, I am nagged by a growing doubt that I have populated my eternity with individuals who may have improper credentials for a Christian heaven. I think I remember envy being a sin, so Salieri may deserve closer scrutiny, and Liszt and Mozart were, in the opinions of some historians, not unfamiliar with the charms and allure of the fairer sex. I feel guilty when I merely pronounce the word "lust", so maybe these guys can't all be in my heaven. Since I personally admire Beethoven so much, I'm not going to thoroughly examine his bonafides, and Ansel Adams probably has living relatives who may be litigious, so he gets a pass.

My point is that I can't conscribe these people to my heaven since their collective eligibility is at least in doubt. Nor does my image include the vexing possibility that I have in constructing my own paradise, inadvertently built a hell for at least one of the players in this drama. What if LVB, hearing restored, is unhappy with Liszt's overly bold interpretation and lunges across the room reaching for his hair to tear him backwards off his bench? What if Salieri, his envy temporarily transformed to desire, dreams of taking young Mozart in his arms and capturing his lips in a man-kiss? Remember the sinful potency of impure thoughts, fellow catechism classmates. To a believer, a healthy libido is oxymoronic.

So the ambiguity of the thing has now corrupted my whole creative process. The hypothetical heaven I posit might work for a few Juilliard students, but Jerry Falwell would be neither happy, nor welcome there.

"Hell is full of musical amateurs; music is the brandy of the damned."

George Bernard Shaw

MAN HEAVEN

Who will demand a heaven for the rough-hewn, deep voiced, hairy-knuckled mouth breathers that populate my gender? Who will speak for stevedores, bouncers, and athletes? If I can temporarily play the part of spokesman for my brothers, I will articulate our requirements for an afterlife.

There must be mountains to climb and clean streams to drink from, fish in, and carry the beer cans downstream. There won't just be flora, they'll be timber (no Bonsai please), and flowers will be merely tolerated (particularly those orchids that are shaped like pudenda). There will be no potpourri or patchouli to foul the range of olfactory stimuli, and the atmosphere should be free of contaminants other than campfire smoke.

Have you watched a baseball player repeatedly raise his glove to his face? He is inspired by the intoxicating mixture of lightly oiled leather, freshly-mown turf, and a hint of horsehide. Throw in the sizzle of fresh bratwurst and beer-stained bleachers and you've got Comiskey Park.

From my experience as a stereotypical guy, I can assure you that my male friends and I will be content with sports to watch, sports to play, and a comfortable place to tell lies about how good we used to be at sports, while quaffing a well chilled beverage.

75

Sentences like "that was a delightful entre-chat" need never be uttered, although spontaneous celebratory dancing may be commonplace.

There will be no membership restrictions to this Eden, although presumably women and gay men will be unimpressed with the accommodations. Visiting lesbians might be a curiosity at first, but the clean-up positions in the batting order of the softball teams will be occupied by these formidable female competitors, and respect will be justly earned.

Since men love things with buttons, it would be nice to have a TV remote that could turn excess pillows and scented candles into deep-fried snacks, with a separate button that could raise and lower the toilet seat in timely anticipation of need.

"If heaven made him, earth can find some use for him."

Chinese Proverb

LADY HEAVEN

Since my first inclination was that lady heaven might be like being the best looking female guard in a male prison, my girlfriend suggested that I might be a bit too dull to understand what would please a woman. The reader is requested to check some of the interviews for supplementary information.

"Ah, women. They make the highs higher and the lows more frequent."

Friedrich Nietzsche

BEST FRIENDS

We are a nation of pet lovers. The billions we spend to feed, groom, and ceremonially inter our beloved poodles and gerbils could eliminate the threat of malaria world-wide within a few years. Love like that should not have to be interrupted by mere mortality, and the overwhelming majority of pet owners would welcome their charges through the pearly gates.

Dogs are far and away the most popular candidates for an afterlife by virtue of their blind love, fidelity, and gratitude. If dogs knew there were people in heaven, they would be hopping up and down and soiling the red carpet with their impatience to be admitted. Cats, on the other hand, would merely feel entitled if not slightly bored by the whole process. One imagines a Noah's Ark type procession of beasts; chittering and grunting their way across the threshold. I would personally draw the line at critters you couldn't cuddle with, effectively eliminating things with bristles, stingers or poisonous fangs[*].

---

[*]There is a noticeable human preference for furry things, which we universally regard as cute (not tarantulas or certain other arachnids). Hairless things (naked mole rats) and things with scales also make some people uncomfortable. If you could grow pink fur on a snake and put a bell on his tail, you would have an adorable pet.

At the risk of sounding discriminatory, I might even exclude a few canines. There must be an alternative residence for those tiny dogs that shake all the time, which might also be too great a temptation to playful carnivores. My heaven will be full of big, clumsy dogs whose eyes are always curious or happy and who slobber when they shake their heads.

If my credentials are insufficient to merit heaven as a man, I might permit myself to be smuggled in a big purse with my head popping out and tongue wagging.

"Are there rewards for doing good to quadrupeds, and giving them water to drink?" Muhammad said,

"Verily there are heavenly rewards for any act of kindness to a live animal."

Prophet Muhammad

INHERITANCE

There are plenty of people, who when pressed to respond to questions about what happens after death, insist that we are the creators of our own heaven or hell, <u>right here on earth</u>. They naively assume that the quality of justice pervades the entire panorama of existence and metes out comfort or pain according to the behavior of the individual. This is clearly the province of self-righteous, healthy, upper middle class people with nice complexions. No starving family automatically assumes that its plight is a consequence of its failure in some unrelated activity. For this unlucky multitude, the guarantee of a single piece of fresh fruit per day would seem like a promise that could only be kept in heaven.

Since it seems likely that the pious have high expectations for their future, the occasional banana will be unlikely to satisfy their dreams of any kind of reward.

Permit me here to interject a memory from Catechism (sort of a seminal religious book for kids) that I think is called a beatitude. "Blessed are the meek, for they shall inherit the earth". I really like this one (there are eight), even though I fear it's too good to be true. Do the meek deserve the cell phones, the ipods, the costume jewelry, the frozen meals, the IRAs, the Ferraris, the leg weights, the sun-block, the wheat grass laxative, the Freon, Styrofoam packing balls, all the plastic crap that produces high pitched electronic noise, and all the haut couture you could stuff into a shipping crate? What do you think the isolated tribes of gentle folk in the rain forest would make of leg weights to make a brisk walk more cardio-challenging? My point is that the meek don't deserve the burden of disposing of all that rubbish even though there is within the beatitude the implicit responsibility for dealing with it on <u>earth</u> (some inheritance).

Now if I could do some of the designing, I think I could take a shot at creating some earthly justice. What if, for example, there were a prison which would only be populated by people who have been proven beyond doubt (I know, I deliberately removed the word reasonable) to have committed a crime with a firearm. The convicted felon would be allowed to bring his (or her) weapon into jail with him. Not only would the staggering costs of long incarcerations dip dramatically, there would be a number of athletic or entertainment options to tempt the odd ghoul or NRA member. Punishment and reward can all be worked into the same design, balancing the books and relieving potential burdens on heaven or hell.

"God has two dwellings: one in heaven, and the other in a meek and thankful heart."
Izaak Walton (1593-1683)

SATAN'S OFFICE

ACT V

Demon: Chief, I've got a great new idea for recreation period!

Satan: I didn't even know we had one. So, amaze me.

Demon: It's something they do on earth. It's called an eating contest. They eat huge amounts of almost any food and the biggest consumer is the winner. You can do it with pickles, clams, pasta, whatever.

Satan: Sounds sickening, what's entertaining about that?

Demon: The people watching take bets on whose meal reverses direction first. The last butter eating contest was won by a guy who was able to keep down five quarter pound sticks. As luck would have it,

	we've got a girl down here who says she can eat six without even chewing.
Satan:	Hmmmm.
Demon:	There's an Asian guy who we're hoping to get who has eaten five dozen hot dogs in six minutes.
Satan:	Hot Dog.... is that some kind of flaming house pet?
Demon:	Not exactly. It's hooves, tails, horns, and lips ground and forced into a pink cylindrical sheath.
Satan (retching):	That's cannibalism!!
	Get out of here before I force your own tail down your throat.

DESIGNER LUNCHES

A sensible heaven must hopefully include the expression of one of the more sublime elements that make life on earth a celebration. I refer, of course, to the two-hour lunch. It may be reasonably contended (by farmers and all-night barmaids) that breakfast should take divine priority, or that dinners, by virtue of their more diverse menus and string quartets are grander, but let's look a bit closer.

The promise of a hearty breakfast would be unlikely to tempt Oscar Wilde or a jazz saxophonist into rising before noon, so the unfortunate early bird may anticipate a cheerfully irritating conversational tone and not a drop of red wine. Moreover, many living humans are more tedious and unattractive in the early hours. Would heaven transform them?

Dinners, on the other hand, frequently represent a daily cyclical completion, accompanied perhaps by fatigue, inebriation, flatulence, and a perfunctory and unenthusiastic attempt at copulation. Dinnertime is a minefield of possible sinful consequences, gluttony being not the least damning.

So, by process of elimination let's pull our chairs out and sit down to the noon meal. Blaise Pascal and Gottfried Leibniz are expected to engage in a lively debate during which Ben Franklin and I will nod our heads sagely over a princely claret and pretend to understand (Heaven is pleasingly challenging). Have no doubts that there is wine in Heaven, or the French would all want to go somewhere else, and a heaven without French influence would be unendurable. Those condemned to everlasting torment might be buoyed by a few bright impressionist blotches and a bit of satire, but if I'm involved in the selection process, I'll be damned if I will permit hell to profit by conscribing my favorite Frenchmen.

Have I failed to mention the carte du jour? Truffles, champagne, pâté, seasonal, fresh, triglycerides, transfats, reptile eggs; your cardiologist is in hell with your lawyer and can't restrict you any more.

But it's not really about the food. The real nourishment in this heaven comes from the entire range of stimuli (if stimuli are absent, I may be overestimating heaven, so just leave me in an urn).

I might invite Ghandi or Madame Curie tomorrow, and I am convinced she would enjoy Bob Marley, who has promised to be here all week. (Heaven obviously has few limitations).

"Heaven, n.: A place where the wicked cease from troubling you with talk of their personal affairs, and the good listen with attention while you expound your own."

Ambrose Bierce

NUMBERS

A friend of mine, who has fallen into the comforting arms of spirituality in his later years, has made a cause of exposing what he believes to be the flaws of evolutionary science. He keeps finding more stuff on the internet to buttress his belief that evolution is a fraud perpetrated by those who would undermine his interpretation of Christianity. His printer works well enough that he can share this information with anyone who is polite enough to accept it, but I think I'm the only one who has read any of it until now.

It's sort of preachy and confusing in general, but to my astonishment there is a startling amount of mathematical justification for Creationism.

The initial premise seemed to suggest that the odds against an event that could set the process of evolution into motion were so great that any reasonable person could dismiss it on that basis. It went something like this: "If you saw someone roll double-ones on a pair of dice ten consecutive times, you could assume that you are in the presence of a cheat." As big numbers go, a two-digit one with a two-digit exponent is not daunting. An event of comparable rarity happens uncountable times every nanosecond somewhere, or possibly everywhere. Scientific interpretations allow for a reasonably large

86

number of possible quantum variations in a universe or a bead of water.

So the anti-evolution argument continues by changing that one in 36^{10} figure into even more impressive numbers, presumably to strike awe into anyone whose calculator only has room for eleven digits*. The incentive for this numerical mumbo-jumbo is to discourage any idea that a strand of genetic material at the perfect moment with proper temperature and gravity, etc. etc., could account for Jessica Simpson.

The only commodity that exceeds the quantity of purported evidence for and against evolution is the contempt the opposing camps have for each other. A just God would slap an atheist on the back and they would have a good chuckle. If your interpretation of science or religion is too narrow, you could be setting yourself up for disappointment. There is a likelihood that you don't know enough about either one to make an informed decision. Even a traditional God shouldn't need to live up to the various interpretations of Scripture‡ or science, nor should evolution be a challenge to all religious beliefs. If I could convince my skeptical friend that at some point prior to, or during the course of evolution, an all-powerful God could have overcome all the troublesome math to impart his divine gift to our little planet, maybe I would let him use the pages of this book to design a hell for evil scientists and mathematicians.

---

*As of this writing, the 45th and 46th Mersenne primes have been identified. The 45th has slightly fewer than 13 million digits and it's just part way to infinity

‡Interestingly, the scientific community credits a 200,000 year old African woman as the earliest known source of human DNA. They call her Eve.

"The danger already exists that the Mathematicians have made a covenant with the devil to darken the spirit and to confine man in the bonds of hell."

Saint Augustine of Hippo

DESIRE

Drug addiction produces the finest line between a perceived paradise and a virtual hell that I have been unlucky enough to witness. Those who haven't had a friend or family member in this dilemma may be quick to dismiss the analogy, but the rest of us have seen the abyss. The attraction of the thrills that some substances provide must be powerful enough to induce otherwise sensible people to trade their souls for an experience that will offer ascendant risk and declining satisfaction.

The transformation of a personality from a superbly responsive social mechanism to a vehicle whose only duty is to maintain the inward flow of intoxicant is chilling. I have looked deeply into the eyes of a good friend only to see the replacement of all other qualities with a lie. The progressive immersion of the junkie into duplicity produces a veil behind which reality can be obscured. Those who are able to deceive themselves have overcome the most significant barrier to shedding the cumbersome burdens of morality, objectivity, and individuality. The consummate liar may elevate his art to its zenith once he has effected this compromise. His full attention can now be given to the numerous enabling opportunities he must seize in his relationships with others. His entire personality becomes an organ, the purpose of which is to remove any impediments to the service of its new master.

What sort of afterlife can an addict expect? Since most of this tragedy is self-inflicted, and the many negative spillover consequences are largely unintended, what punishment would be appropriate?

Rehab is a perfect analogy for purgatory. Pain and suffering would be dominant, but even with the coaxing of chittering therapists, and the balm of Gospel floggers, deliverance may be possible. Would a self-respecting addict, given the choice, willingly submit to a term of ferocious cleansing, or would he just say "the hell with it" and leap into the inferno? If the freedom to choose could be extended beyond mortality, perhaps this spiritually barren segment of the population could be given one more chance. Heaven may seem initially dreary, but you probably can't score a dime bag in hell either.

"Those who restrain desire, do so because theirs is weak enough to be restrained."
William Blake (1757-1827)
"The Marriage of Heaven and Hell"

CLEANLINESS IS NEXT TO GODLINESS

From my perspective (hypochondriac, germophobe, etc. etc.), cleanliness is a most worthy and basic aspiration, and should entitle those who achieve it to an eternal carte blanche. People who disinfect, exfoliate, and scrub 'til the washcloth is bloody are the noblest of nature's gifts and should be rewarded accordingly. There's a reason heaven is always depicted in shades of joyful white, and you just know it smells like a fresh pine detergent with a dash of lemon.

Conversely, hell is likely to fall a bit short of that ideal. When I imagine "dirty", I don't see topsoil or canal water; I picture gelatinous, malodorous, filamentous, infectious slime. I see it running in rivers and clinging to the sides of caves and mobile homes, overwhelming and nauseating. I see it vividly on the hands of people who emerge from a bathroom where I can't hear the reassuring sound of running water. If someone coughs into a handkerchief, I instinctively assume that he is on a break from his occupation as food server or surgical nurse.

If I cannot wash up very soon after shaking hands* with an old friend or new acquaintance, I will begin to convulse. And going camping is totally out of the question. People just relax their most admirable habits a little too much.

Now I'm not saying carelessly dirty people should fry in an unsanitary kind of burning hell. Lots of saints probably weren't that clean, and no religion I am aware of condemns the filthy, but they should be carefully disinfected before being admitted to the pristine Eden that we deserve.

"If there is, in fact, a Heaven and a Hell, all we know for sure is that Hell will be a viciously over-crowded version of Phoenix...."
  Hunter S. Thompson (1939-2005), Generation of Swine

---

*I am delighted to report the inevitable spread of the fist bump as a gesture of sportsmanship or congratulation within the arena of athletic competition. This worldwide phenomenon is a welcome replacement for the hand shake, which, when wet with perspiration, can be sickeningly intimate, or the various high and low fives, which white people are incapable of properly executing.

INTERVIEW WITH A GOURMET

The poorest people in the world worry about where their next meal will come from. As median prosperity ascends, so will attention to quality, convenience, and health benefits. When you finally reach the point in your life that "eating" becomes "dining", you may be forsaking other opportunities in exchange for the planning, purchasing, sharing and savoring of meals. At this moment you have made an implicit contract with the devil to exchange brain cells for taste buds. Although this may seem harsh, I offer the following guidelines to salvation:

1. Your first dinner date should be special. Breakfast should be healthful.
2. Taking nourishment should produce a net energy gain, not the other way around.
3. Never sit at a meal for more than 40 minutes unless the conversation is extremely stimulating or if you are pitching a new product.
4. Be cautious about dining etiquette*, it can be lethal.

---

*The story of the great sixteenth century astronomer Tycho Brahe's death-by-banquet has been told for hundreds of years. It is said he refused to empty his bladder before the meal was formally concluded for fear of offending his host. He died of infection eleven days later.

5. Never eat or drink so much that romance would be uncomfortable.
6. Don't spend more money on truffles and paté than you give to charity.

I spoke at length with a friend of generous proportions (5'11, 465 lbs), and not surprisingly his ideas of heaven centered on food. Although he admitted to a skeptical outlook about any kind of afterlife, even the most jaded cynic may harbor a flicker of hope. His heaven consists of the stewardship and influence of 200 years of France's most famous chefs, preparing their specialties, and consulting with him afterwards on how they might improve a particular dish. The fictional Nero Wolfe would nod his head approvingly. When pressed to conceive of hell, his response was a bit surprising. He wasn't afraid of any biblical hell (being well insulated against heat, perhaps) nor was he, as you might suppose, concerned about starvation or emaciation. His greatest fear was an eternity of badly prepared dishes!

I imagine him writhing in agony as he is forced to consume an overcooked crepe or a paella with too much salt, fiendishly accompanied by a questionable German wine served at room temperature. Condemnation to an eternity of this kind of disappointment may not sound too dire to you, but there were genuine tears in his eyes as he described this latter fate.

"My kitchen is a mystical place, a kind of temple for me. It is a place where the surfaces seem to have significance, where the sounds and odors carry meaning that transfers from the past and bridges to the future"

Pearl Mae Bailey

"My idea of heaven is eating pate de foie gras to the sound of trumpets."

Sydney Smith

SATAN'S OFFICE

ACT VI

Demon:	Got a minute, chief?
Satan:	Make it quick. I've got a pedicure appointment in twelve minutes.
Demon:	Well, it's a bit confusing. It seems a hot tub exploded and started a mudslide that swept a funny-shaped building into the ocean.
Satan:	Don't tell me. California, right?
Demon:	You've got a gift, chief. Anyway, this odd group of people presented themselves to Saint Peter without proper credentials or testimony. They call themselves Scientologists.
Satan:	Is that with a P or an S?
Demon:	I don't know, but Saint Peter couldn't understand a word

they were saying. They seemed arrogant and evasive, so he sent 'em here.

Satan: Why do humans have to constantly create grotesque new systems to dedicate their lives to?

Demon: Beats me. What are we supposed to do with 'em?

Satan: Have we still got that Kohoutek crowd spinning in that mock space ship?

Demon: Yup. That was one great design. Those suckers thought a comet/space ship would transport them to bliss. Instead, centrifugal force is pinning them to the walls of their so-called craft while they puke their guts out. Be careful what you wish for, eh chief?

Satan: Do you think the psychologists would enjoy the Kohoutek people?

Demon: It's a match made in heaven. And by the way, it's Scientologists chief.

Satan: Whatever. Send a message to Saint Peter that we're not a

clearing-house for his discards.
We have standards to uphold.

Demon: We got pride too, don't we chief?

Satan: My favorite sin; now start
            enlarging that flying saucer
            and see if you can get it spin-
            ning faster.

Demon: I'm on it, chief.

EXORCISM

There are uncountable instances in which divine influences on earthly events have been documented. Visitation, transubstantiation, intercession, bleeding statuary, toast with holy images on it, Styrofoam burned by microwave into a holy shape, and miracles too numerous to mention suggest the existence of a mysterious corridor between heaven and earth.

Apparently, there is evidence, though not quite so abundant, to suggest occasional visitations from representatives of the other place. Demons, witches, banshees, and poltergeists have flickered briefly in and out of notice for millennia. Folklore and literature chronicle a variety of colorful examples of fiendish character, but the footprints have grown faint in the harsh light of the electronic age. When these beings emerge with their sulphurous breath, typically they are dealt with by a saint, a priest, or a brave knight who utters words like: "begone demon" or "I hereby expel thee back to thy grim master", or "prithee knave, hie thee hence." This technique has worked so well that heads almost never rotate 360° upon the torso anymore.

Nearly all the world's religions, including the Hollywood film industry, have utilized the attention given to incidents that challenge the righteous to deal with the damned. If you want to fill the pews, just hire a couple of professional twitchers and scream loud prayers at them.

If I could capture a real life exorcist and press him into servitude, I would drag him behind me until I saw evidence of demonic influence, then I would point and say "Do him".

Imagine a freeway driver dawdling along in the far left lane 10 miles per hour below the limit, blithely engaged in animated conversation on her* mobile phone while other drivers maneuver around frantically to avoid the ensuing bottleneck. If we could perform a class action exorcism, millions of drivers would throw their phones out the window with the dazed look of people newly awakened from their dreams. "My God!" they might say: "What was I thinking?" This Quixotic mission could logically be extended to address other potentially diabolical habits pre-need, as in cemetery plots. It seems a shame to waste all this righteousness.

"What power would Hell have if those imprisoned there were not able to dream of Heaven?"
                                                                    Neil Gaiman

---

*Female drivers going under the speed limit in the passing lane while using a phone outnumber males in the same category by a margin of four to one. (I kept a journal for 11 months until my girlfriend ripped it up).

POLITICAL REWARDS (GOP)

Imagine a perfect clear day in a forest in September, a bracing 68 degree 5 knot breeze off the lake, and the expected wildlife (not too wild) capering under the mature trees. Consider now the enhancement of this Eden with the addition of eighteen 500 yard swaths of fertilized, perfectly manicured, genetically ideal fairway; scientifically engineered to guarantee that a dimpled ball will roll long and true. Add an Olympic size pool, a few har-tru tennis courts, and a world class restaurant, and you have created an institution that may rival or exceed heaven's questionable bounty. About this restaurant, don't expect the shrimp to have shells or veins (a euphemism), nor will any kind of turkey sausage be available, but the wine list will exceed all earthly expectations. The conversation will be subdued, and will largely revolve around how best to respond to the imagined hardships of the lower castes. (This might imply the presence of Hindus in the clubroom but they are not likely to be voted on this year).

Sounds pretty sweet, right?

Well, with a few miniscule changes, Arcadia may be transformed. Picture if you will, the addition of a handful of multi-colored children casting their vile effluent into the pool, and a dread-locked waiter giv-

ing a founding member a little uppity; and the re-
newal drive will be a failure, with the whole place
going public in six months. There's some moral justification for Democrats voting "Caddyshack" one of
the greatest sports movies of all time.

The margin between heaven and hell is very narrow at some points.

(A LITTLE TO THE LEFT)

Where will good Democrats go when they shuttle
off their mortal coils? I have a dream. It is of a perfect sunset, only partially obscured by rows of not
unpleasant co-operative buildings. The adequate
window in each cubicle will have an excellent view of
the benzene-free river below, where fish thrive and
the water is nearly drinkable. The restful and me-
lodic voices of NPR commentators issue from every
hallway and doors are open in anticipation of the
food delivery which happens almost every day. The
heart of this paradise is the common area below,
where the residents assemble to share their optimism with one another over chessboards, in yoga
classes, and at poetry readings. Their satisfaction
comes from milling about with pipe-smokers and
Bantu chiefs, congresswomen and sommeliers, bank
tellers and bikini wax specialists, all nattering away
about Chopin or Nietzsche like a bunch of commu-
nisti at an olive festival. The expectation of
everlasting comfort and ease is apparently secondary to the anticipation of engagement with one's
fellow man.

The unlucky Republican who happened to blunder into this mélange would assume his patron saint had abandoned him. He would see the impassioned faces with intelligent welcoming eyes, and become catatonic with fear that the little stroll he was taking with his purebred miniatures had led him to the gates of hell.

Other affiliations will have to be absorbed into the two-party system since heaven, hell, and this essay have neither the latitude, nor the necessity to accommodate too much political diversity.

"Paradise is nearer to you than the thongs of your sandals; and the Fire likewise."

Prophet Muhammad

KEEP THE FAITH

No quality imparts apparent strength to its possessor more effectively than faith. From hospital beds to battlefields, it is the iron that strengthens a man to confront his destiny.

The umbrella that faith provides shelters a lot of diversity however, and what seems despicable about one man's beliefs may be admirable to another.

National Public Radio aired a story in 2008 that had been well covered by the print media, but never of headline stature. In Iraq, earlier in the occupation, or pacification, or whatever one chooses to call a debacle, the American military had begun a training program for militia and police trainees. These young Iraqi men had been lured from behind the counters of their shops and desks by the promise of a regular paycheck, which indicates the extent of their familiarity with weapons.

After a little training, a group of these brave but inexperienced men who spoke no English were left in an unsettled neighborhood with a translator and a few American instructors. When, inevitably, the sound of gunfire was heard nearby, a number of the trainees ran to a six foot wall, raised their guns over the top, and fired blindly into the surrounding area until an Iraqi translator, enthusiastically prompted by the Americans, bade them cease fire.

When asked to explain their dangerous fusillade, one man responded; "If it is the will of Allah, the bullet will find an enemy." (A linguistic approximation due to translation difficulties and the passage of time). I am in no position to grasp the will of Allah, but I would be uncomfortable with the interpretation of his words that I might get from a man holding a gun. The devout should pray for the separation of religion and weapons, since some of the world's great crimes have been committed in the name of God.

There are those who believe God whispers into their ears to bomb a clinic that terminates pregnancies, or to invade a country to introduce democracy, or whatever. The validity of a number of sensible causes may be poisoned by the danger of confusing a misinterpretation of God's will with sound judgment. Fanaticism, in any of its flavors is such an egregious celebration of vanity that it should be prosecutable in the afterlife.

By degree, those Iraqi trainees seem less culpable than most. Those responsible for the cruelty of the inquisition, or the crusades, or any other misdirected faith based initiative, are hopefully boring each other to distraction in the nether realm. The kind of faith I admire doesn't come spewing out to offend anyone unlucky enough to be in its proximity. Give me the clear-eyed pragmatist any day. His faith may strengthen his inner qualities of justice, humility, charity, and even intellect, and these traits can reflect back on his spiritual beliefs to fortify them. Gandhi and Mother Teresa effectively changed the lives of millions of people without ever throwing a bomb or using faith as a bludgeon. Heaven should trot out John Philip Sousa to write a march for their welcome.

"To enter heaven, a man must take it with him."
Unknown

SEX

Sex is such a sensitive subject for some people; I almost couldn't overcome my reluctance to volunteer an opinion. Within the context of my overall theme, sex represents an ambiguous challenge. Ignoring the strictly biological aspects of the activity, it is widely believed that sex can be responsible for your eligibility to be interviewed by his infernal highness. However, plenty of us would behave differently on earth if we knew there would be tactile recreation in heaven.

I don't want to get ahead of myself, or treat this topic with less than the delicacy it deserves, but I warn the reader to prepare for opinions that will be free of the tedium of clinical accuracy or ethical consistency.

In order to narrow the focus of this modest effort I have arbitrarily eliminated from consideration the most loathsome practices that may occur in the minds of deviants or the pages of police reports.

Though I'm sure there are no dearth of voices to defend abominations like pedophilia or sex which is not consensual, I hope that the ears that must endure them come to a point at the top. Exclusively procreative sex, and the kind of obligatory sex that must be enacted in order to fulfill the marriage contract, fall well outside my meager experience, thus will be given short shrift here.

Since the hope of any kind of sex in hell would undermine morality on earth, and enlarge the population of hell beyond any reasonable capacity, it may be assumed that its residents will have to content themselves with other diversions. If we concede the complete and punitive absence of sex in Satan's jurisdiction, may we logically infer its possible utility as a reward in heaven?

If we can acknowledge the just and elegant balance of such an assumption, then we tacitly accommodate the possibility of heavenly sex. It may be hoped that there exists an environment in which passion, love, desire and fulfillment interchangeably function within the same exquisite act. Without the ubiquitous guilt that centuries of cultural and religious influence have rightly or wrongly imposed on it, we may learn to soar with the abandon of angels.

I have a vague fear that defining sex within such a nugatory context as I can provide may be an unjustly narrow portrayal, but I am undeterred. I am, merely, a heterosexual, middle-aged white guy who is trying to sell his opinions in books, so here goes.

(In order to counterfeit objectivity, avoid self-incrimination, discourage litigation, and justify exaggeration under the guise of artistic license, I narrate this single presentation in the third person singular.)

Her touch could not have seared his skin since they were still separated by several feet, but his pulse and breathing reacted as if he were already swimming in the scented heat of her body. What they saw in each other's eyes might have produced a loss of equilibrium if their focus had been less intense. Their unspoken commitment to that anticipated moment was growing and uneven. It was hunger only briefly to be tamed by patience. It was selfless and needful in a tidal way. It demanded and conceded in the same instant. It was wild promise married to understatement, deafening murmurs and unheard screams; and all before they had touched.

Their unspoken agreement said "I will take, and I will give. I promise we will never forget what has preceded this moment, and what will follow it. The distant past is as the distant future. They are nothing."

The space between them closed, but neither was conscious of movement; in the way of familiar dancers who respond gracefully to the subtlest cues.

She placed her hand gently on the soft flesh inside his hip and smiled as his back arched involuntarily in response. He vainly tried to regain eye contact, but hers were nearly closed in an erotic thrall so he contented himself with regarding her breast, not to admire its graceful contour, but to watch her respiration shorten with passion, and live it with her. There were long moments when she could not tell whether it was his tongue, his breath, or his fingertip that inflamed her hungry body. She, in turn, found a spot on his long torso that made him tremble, left it, and visited it again only after she had found another. No amorous contract demands reciprocity but joyfully, it arrives unbidden.

The rhythm of their desire slowly but inevitably fell into ecstatic synchrony as their bodies demanded more and more closeness, as no physical or emotional barrier remained intact; and they discovered together every nerve ending, every pore, from the exterior to the throbbing heart of their unified form. Michelangelo never tried to capture such an image in marble, but with all his genius, he could not have offered a hint of its perfection.

No single climactic event separated itself from the turbulence to which they were committed. There was simply no moment that did not have the character of physical release. They fell limp, then rigid once more until fatigue overcame them.

"Of the delights of this world, man cares most for sexual intercourse, yet he has left it out of his heaven."
                                                            Mark Twain

POSTSCRIPT TO SEX
(AFTERGLOW)

Upon reflection, I fear I may have clumsily slipped into the fields of romance or pornography, but since the previous essay was the product of impulse rather than inspiration, I offer the following rationalization. I believed the source of my effort was a spasm, not an idea. A bad idea might lead to the creation of a crappy book. It doesn't even have to be my bad idea; there are a great many to plagiarize. A versatile talent could even turn someone else's good idea into a crappy book.

In the genre of romance, one merely takes an impulse like mine and decorates it with a few thousand words like passion, hunger, castle, inflamed, codpiece, and glistening; toss in a few prepositions, and voilá, literature! Satan's bookstore will feature thousands of titles, complete with gaudy cover art, but every book will be identical. My pragmatic aspiration is to write a not too crappy book that won't be a mirror image of someone else's. I will try to govern my impulses more closely in the future.

SATAN'S OFFICE

ACT VII

Demon: We have confusion in admissions again.

Satan: Is there no end to the incompetence?

Demon: I've got some people in new arrivals that defy classification.

Satan: In what way?

Demon: We can't tell whether they're men or women chief.

Satan: Just give them the joke test. It's well known that women can't respond to humor due to faulty DNA, so make a fart noise and see who laughs. Women think babies and kittens are hilarious but they don't laugh at flatulence. Can you imagine?

Demon: We tried that chief, but they all looked like they were sneering or smirking. There was no clear response.

Satan: Humans are apparently still evolving. We'll have to try the spit test.

Demon: I never heard of that one.

Satan: That's why you're not the boss. A man can spit through the window of a car going seventy, and think nothing of it. Have you seen a female try to spit?

Demon: No, come to think of it.

Satan: The only place it happens is in the bathroom. As a woman brushes her teeth, for instance, she closes the door for privacy. Now she stares at the mirror like a dog concentrating on a refrigerator door, making sure that her hips and shoulders are properly positioned, and moves her hair out of harm's way. Then, she makes kind of a sputtering noise and hopes for gravity to work its

	magic, but her chin will always be in the way*.
Demon:	It sounds absurd.
Satan:	I highly recommend it for entertainment. Now get back up there with some toothpaste.
Demon:	Aye-Aye, chief.

---

*I can, from personal experience, corroborate Satan's observations. A woman once crossed a room to spit in my face (case of mistaken identity), and I took grim notice of the event. She launched angrily at me, and while some of the fluid found its mark, sixty percent of the intended projectile morphed into a viscous gobbet that swung precariously between her chin and her breast, thus relieving the tension in the room.

My girlfriend asked what could have precipitated such an event. I said, hypothetically, perhaps a girl might become that angry if someone inadvertently slept with someone's best friend or twin sister. Some people lack self-control.

CRUISIN'

Some familiar activities have the potential to simultaneously produce elation and misery depending on perspective. I know people, for example, who are positively giddy about exercise and all its attendant joys. My poker buddies on the other hand, would run for the medicine cabinet for something to counteract the effects of an endorphin. I spent hours trying to imagine a single situation that would be heavenly for some, and hellish for the rest of us, and I couldn't pry my imagination away from one concept, the Caribbean Cruise. Don't doubt that a fair number of folks, if promised an eternal cruise in lieu of heaven, would be racing out to purchase Dramamine and jaunty cruise wear. Oh sure, it sounds great. The starry skies and breathtaking sunsets over the ocean have the power to bring us emotionally closer to paradise than any thing in my humble experience.

There is so much more to consider, however. These luxury ships are actually floating refrigerators and dining rooms designed to appeal to people who set their alarms for 1:00 AM so they don't miss the fourth daily meal. And did I mention it's all free. Consider your fellow clientele at a restaurant where you could eat unlimited amounts of excellent food at no cost. The sounds of subdued conversation would be overwhelmed by the brutish snuffling and slurping. Oh, I know, that's not all there is to it. You can always go ashore and have your hair braided into dreadlocks that send the friendly natives into fits of laughter as you waddle proudly away. Or perhaps you can visit the fantail where the speed and direction of the ship can straighten out that slice that the guys in the clubhouse have been snickering about for decades.

The worst characteristic of the cruise, however, is the frequency of unwanted contact. It doesn't really matter whether you are trying not to appear rude, or you are merely repelled by your shipmates. The number of places you can hide will rapidly diminish until you are reduced to praying for landfall in your cabin. There, you will be contriving a strategy to maroon yourself on some mosquito-infested islet.

Hollywood is responsible for all the increased exposure this appalling pastime receives. Remember that daffy cast on TV's "Loveboat" or maybe the tear-jerking "Titanic". Cruising has the potential to be grim even without all the eating.

The cinematic triumph for this genre, however, is "The Poseidon Adventure". Here, one may find threats sufficient to constitute genuine horror. The ship, as you may recall, turns upside down so the unlucky passengers are exposed to the dangers of drowning, suffocation, and claustrophobia. All this and Shelly Winters too. Add the twenty-first century bonus of highly contagious diarrheic illness, and consider all those upside down toilets and holding tanks and you've got yourself a real thriller.

Bon Voyage!

"Travel has no longer any charm for me. I have seen all the foreign countries I want to except heaven & hell & I have only a vague curiosity about one of those."

Mark Twain

REINCARNATION

With the exception of one notable event, most Christians don't consider an earthly tenure beyond a few decades. Millions of non-Christians, however, believe the reward for a righteous lifetime is rebirth as a higher form.

If merit determines placement in the reincarnate hierarchy, then I could be in for an unpleasant future. I may aspire to the robes of an archbishop or the adulation of millions for my performances of Shakespearean drama, but the merit system probably entitles me to a more realistic continuation, perhaps as a lichen, a coral polyp*, or one of my dim-witted friends.

Thanks to an arrogant and selfish past, I may not have enough time to accumulate the necessary credits to be eligible for promotion, so I must put my eggs in another basket.

One trip to the confessional and ba-da-bing, the ugly self portrait is transformed into an expectant cherub, awaiting his wings and halo.

I pray that whoever is doing the sorting recognizes my potential as a comedian.

---

*I know what your thinking, but I don't think rebirth as an intestinal polyp is realistic.

117

"Heaven goes by favour. If it went by merit, you would stay out and your dog would go in."

Mark Twain (1835-1910)

THE DAMNED?

Since my frame of reference is specific to the faith I grew up with, certain ideas my fellow Catholics and I have been exposed to may seem alien to those not similarly indoctrinated.

Suicide, like murder, is deemed to be mortally sinful by Catholics everywhere. Since only sacramental confession can offer hope of absolution from sin, including murder, suicide by definition removes any hope of subsequent confessional relief, thus: suicide = hell.

My sense of non-religious justice strains to assign a different level of punishment for those who take their own lives due to persistent severe, chronic pain, and those who commit serial murder. Hell is apparently just plain old non-discriminating hell.

Is it possible some non-corporeal Vincent Van Gogh (suicide) and Marilyn Monroe (possible suicide) are sitting with Ernest Hemingway (suicide) in a bar in a place like Scranton in mid-winter? Hemingway is bitching about watered-down rum and stale appetizers to Ms. Monroe, and she couldn't be more bored. She would like to talk to Vincent, but his head is between his hands and he is crying. Perhaps nature doesn't present her brightest colors here, so there's nothing to sketch. Liquor is an insufficient antidote to bitterness of this magnitude.

I cannot endure the thought of Ted Bundy or Joseph Stalin kibitzing with the band in the same place. Surely, they deserve worse, and that's where the fun part comes up. There could be a board game whose goal would be the design of a winning hell. Matching crime to punishment would not only be great fun, it could be agreeably cautionary to the kiddies. Let's look at Stalin; an accomplished murderer whose utter indifference to the suffering he inflicted on a scale beyond imagination's scope qualifies him, I assume for special treatment. One single anecdote, believed attributable to him, exemplifies his sangfroid. When he was approached by a subordinate who urged him not to execute members of an ethnic group whom he had marked for extermination, he was reminded that they had served him faithfully and helped in his quest for influence. His simple response was: "Gratitude is a disease of dogs", which simultaneously discolors humanity, canines, and the gentle quality of gratitude.

What would be the apt punishment for such a fiend? Force feeding him his least favorite vegetable while hip-hop lyrics are set to a country music score at maximum volume 24/7 seems incomprehensibly cruel, but even that can be exceeded. If you have access to a thousand interchangeable hells, it may be possible to concoct a more balanced and satisfying place of eternal torment. To do this correctly, one must reject the time-honored image of a flaming inferno, replete with sharp-featured red bipeds herding bookies and showgirls from cavern to cauldron. Any Hollywood screenwriter could do better for Pete's sake.

Hell should be as uniquely perfect as heaven, as vague or precise as metaphysics would dictate. The concept of relativity could establish equal and opposite in the afterlife in ways Einstein (heaven probably) might approve of.

"Who would fardels bear, to grunt and sweat under a weary life, but that the dread of something after death, the undiscover'd country from whose bourn no traveler returns, puzzles the will, and makes us rather bear those ills we have than fly to others that we know not of?"

William Shakespeare

THE ADRENAL GLAND

There is a broad category of individuals whose earthly contentment seems to revolve around exciting, edgy, sometimes morally questionable behaviors. The stimuli provided therein could cram emergency rooms with cardiac events if normal humans were exposed to them. I refer, of course, to pastimes like skydiving, ski jumping, luge, unsafe sex, racy novels, no-limit hold'em, and options trading.

How are the practitioners of such gut-wrenching hobbies going to endure eternity in their absence? Not only are they likely to become fractious with the paralyzing serenity of heaven, they will quickly lose patience with the other residents. Imagine a couple of crack-smoking stockbrokers locked in a room with a herd of proselytizing cult members. Before too long, the floor would be covered with shredded robes and shattered Rolexes.

This example is exaggerated for the sake of contrast, but let's face it; a lot of us need a little action. Could we possibly petition the almighty to reserve a small corner of heaven for white-water rafting down a river that leads into a town with a casino? Sammy, Frank and Dino will be in the lounge, and since heaven is just, they'll be doing requests. They're all hoping Wayne Newton will live forever because they fear he'll want all the dressing rooms and the pent-house suite for himself.

Now some of you may be finding this interpretation a bit narrow. Shouldn't the ministers of hell be allowed to present a bid for this concession? Who do you think could provide a better rush; Sam Giancana or Mohandas Gandhi? Does your girlfriend dream about Branson, Missouri, or Las Vegas? The obstacle to all this wishful thinking is that what might be perfectly natural in Vegas, like lap dances and casino hostesses, could be frowned upon in most versions of heaven. I have a compromise solution. Since losing anything of value would be moot in heaven's gaming parlors, the players could only break even or win.

What might be worth winning in heaven? Let's say you could win temporary crossover passes to that other casino, the one where the thrills exceed a run on the dime slots and a second dessert at the all-night buffet. Leaving the details to the eternally damned might provide just the adrenal challenge to satisfy the busloads of grannies who thought Chippendale's was furniture. After a few millennia of harp solos and poetry readings, people might be relieved to see a lesbian kiss between Siegfried and Cher.

Thanks to their deep immersion in counterfeit realities like dungeons and dragons or fantasy football, some folks will be dissatisfied with most of heaven's options. The smell of fresh dew or greenery just can't compete with lasing the guts out of warlocks, or having your star player get ten sacks in a playoff game. Alas, eternity isn't constructed of pixels and electronic grunts and screams. There may be the odd fairy or unicorn to harass, but if you think you can go around stalking things with fangs or claws; forget it. They're in the bad place.

Perhaps it would be possible to petition the highly placed to consent to the creation of an occasional safari, where restless souls could visit the nether regions and pot raptors and villains with the weapon of their choice. Naturally, the taking of trophies or meat for the freezer would be discouraged, but as on earth, exaggeration will be not only tolerated, but welcome. Tales of slaughter are generally tedious unless the dimensions and numbers of victims exceed those of previous instances.

As long as we are expanding hell's identity into a flexible kind of location, why not provide a few additional amenities to amuse the righteous tourists? On the border between hell and not hell, we could use a few good honky-tonks and a topless joint. A couple of long necks and a lap dance might be a pleasant way to get the smell of cordite out of your nostrils after an entertaining afternoon of slaying demons and whatnot.

"Nothing is too high for the daring of mortals: we storm heaven itself in our folly."
Quintus Horatius Flaccus Horace

MURRAY'S PECULIAR DREAM

I have, in the writing of this book, depended upon many opinions to illustrate the nature of a heaven. Dreams should be honored here as well, since they are no less valid than most opinions of an entity about which so little is known. This particular borrowed dream somehow links earth and heaven, childhood and maturity.

I was, as a young man, often invited to the residence of two friends, Timothy and Richard, who lived a life, it seemed to me, of splendid leisure. I could always depend on the presence of poets and philosophers from all over the world to provide the nourishment that the sumptuous picnics, for which my hosts were well known, did not. Exotic fruits, giant artichokes, grapes in every form (fermented and aged), nougats of chocolate and too much more to recount, comprised the table. The events however were always dwarfed by the setting, which could have been the product of a magician's wand.

Their house was grand, or perhaps ordinary, since it was overwhelmed by the surrounding landscape which has partially dissolved my memory of any man-made structure. The part of the estate which bordered the road was decorated by an exquisitely simple, low fence which could hardly have prevented an intruder from coming in or a resident from departing, although I witnessed neither occurence. It was apparently a margin conferred by a sort of mutual acknowledgement.

The distance between fence and horizon was impossibly large even for this pastoral acreage, and was populated by some extraordinary denizens. On that horizon, which constantly recedes as all must, one may discern enormous herds of some grazing animal which I call the not-quites. They aren't gnu or wildebeest, neither eland nor kudu, and can never be approached since they graze only where the sun appears to set. Since I can't quite ever get close enough, and I'm not quite that familiar with all the possibilities, I call them thus.

Somewhere between the not-quites and the fence roam a number of fierce-looking but indifferent pigs. They seem neither hostile nor curious about humans, though I haven't tried to stroke ones back yet. They may be partially responsible for the effectiveness of the fence however, as no visitor unfamiliar with their gentle nature would dare to cross over.

Not the least fascinating of the creatures within the boundaries, the next are likely to challenge the most vivid imagination.

They are flying pink toys. Yes I said toys! They are not dolls or GI Joes, or even X-Boxes, but simple round, soft, fluttering faceless cottony spheres and cones roughly the size of dinnerware. Their nature is quite playful and social to the extent that their familiarity can be a slight nuisance at picnics, for instance, where they may tip over a glass of ale or fall into the Waldorf salad. They are noiseless hovering little beings with the audacity of puppies that require attention and diversion. I hesitate to use the word swarm, as it may recall memories of mosquitoes or wasps, but this is roughly how they conduct themselves and thus create a kind of benign confusion wherever they assemble. These toys, as I have said are relatively small, since, as everyone is aware, the force of gravity will bring a large pink toy crashing to earth in no time at all.

The single unchanging element in this odd menagerie is the total commitment to the light of day. When the sun sets, all evidence of sound or motion seems to vanish. No scuttling, no roaring, twittering, howling or trumpeting disrupts the patient darkness. It is not the darkness of a tomb or pit, however. It is more like the darkness of a young child's closet as he prepares to sleep. In other words, it is at once hopeful and vaguely threatening, but never final.

Having spent one exceptional afternoon in this remarkable place, I returned then, in the failing light, to the house which now seemed much smaller to bid my hosts good night. Upon arriving, I was alarmed to note that both Timothy and Richard had aged terribly! They seemed incapable of addressing their own needs, moving uncertainly, clumsily, and implausibly confused by the coming of night. I gently showed them to their separate quarters and thanked them for the perfect day which they seemed not to recall, and then, satisfied with their comfort, I took my leave.

As I returned to my world, one of cars and buses and alarm clocks, I remembered suddenly that I had forgotten the key to my own modest dwelling and decided to retrace my steps.

As I re-entered the fenced property, I noticed that the house that I had left dark was now illuminated, and seemed to announce its own sense of purpose and being (this observation depends exclusively, of course, on one's imagination).

Upon knocking, I became aware instantly of the stroke of bow on string that was not quite Beethoven and not quite Mozart, but something original. I walked through the door to see Richard, his gnarled hands capably producing an etude of unimaginable richness and complexity. He indicated with a nod of his head another room where Timothy, with great lusty brush strokes was creating something not quite unlike impressionism, but altogether like a masterwork, in which he had captured all the animating light of the previous day and imprisoned it upon his canvas.

I thought it could not be the same pair that I had so recently shown to bed, but before my eyes their combined genius was performing some kind of magical rejuvenation, and it was not hard to see that they would be completely re-invigorated by sunrise. I was dizzy with the awareness that I had lived so long in ignorance of such miracles, and understood that there might be a good deal more beyond the reach of my shallow ability to reason. Timothy and Richard continued their passionate creation as I fell into a half-sleep with exhaustion. Images of pointillist pigs and pink geometry lessons chased me through my half-dreams as not quite Mozart produced the rhythm for our collective movement. My subsequent reflections on this evening demonstrated no clear boundary between what is dreamt and what is real, however, I'm sure I heard Richard and Timothy, young and smooth again, chattering good-naturedly on what to pack for that day's picnic.

There is a sort of mental treason
that smothers dreams outside of reason.

SATAN'S OFFICE

ACT VIII

Demon: Hey chief, sorry to disturb you, but there's a guy named Murray with a visitor's pass that wants to say hello.

Satan: Is he a goth or a warlock?

Demon: No. He says he's an engineer.

Satan: I love trains.

Demon: Not that kind of engineer; you know, like in construction.

Satan: Send him in. Maybe he can design something to torture people better.

Demon: (returning) Murray, Satan. Satan, Murray.

Murray: Dude (he bumps fists with Satan).

Satan:	(still looking at his hand) Charmed. Can I do something for you?
Murray:	I wondered what I could get for my immortal soul?
Satan:	I'll tell you what. Help me come up with something that will make people sick and want to tear out their hair, and I'll let you keep your sorry little soul.
Murray:	And in exchange, I get what?
Satan:	You get to keep your lungs and penis you idiot. Who did you think you were bargaining with?
Murray:	I have access to something that fits your needs to a tee. My friend Mike wrote it, and it invariably produces nausea.
Satan:	You've got a deal. I'll take 10,000 of them.
Murray:	Dude (they bump fists).

(Exeunt)

BIBLIOGRAPHY

The Kentucky Democrat, Wednesday, November 16, 2005

Smithsonian Magazine, April 2008, Avis Berman "Larger than Life"

Giordano Bruno: The Forgotten Philosopher, John J. Kessler

A Regrettable Life: Tomas de Torquemada, Beth Randall © 1996

Raoul Wallenberg, Biography, Jan Larsson and The International Raoul Wallenberg Foundation

Great Internet Mersenne Prime Search, Oct/Nov/Dec 2008

ABOUT THE AUTHOR

Mike Corbett has spent most of his life on and around Fort Lauderdale beach, where he and his friends used to sell their blood for beer money.